C000145696

International Develop
Challenges for a World in Transition

Introduction to

SUSTAINABILITY

Prepared for the Course Team by Gordon Wilson, with contributions
from Stephen Peake and Pam Furniss

Cover photo: Taxi drivers block traffic on the highway out of Charles de Gaulle airport in Roissy, north of Paris, 7 September 2000. Taxi drivers joined truckers and farmers in their protest against rising fuel prices.

The Open University
Walton Hall
Milton Keynes
MK7 6AA
United Kingdom

First published 2001

Copyright © 2001 The Open University

All rights reserved. No part of this publication may be reproduced, stored in a retrieval system, or transmitted in any form or by any means without written permission from the publisher or without a licence from the Copyright Licensing Agency Limited. Details of such licences (for reprographic reproduction) may be obtained from the Copyright Licensing Agency Ltd, 90 Tottenham Court Road, London W1P 0LP

Edited, designed and typeset by The Open University

Printed in the United Kingdom by The Alden Group, Oxford

ISBN 0 7492 3812 7

This publication forms part of an Open University course U213 *International Development: Challenges for a World in Transition*

Details of this and other Open University courses can be obtained from the Call Centre, PO Box 724, The Open University, Milton Keynes, MK7 6ZS, United Kingdom, tel. +44 (0)1908 653231, email ces-gen@open.ac.uk. Alternatively, you may visit the Open University website at http://www.open.ac.uk where you can learn more about the wide range of courses and packs offered at all levels by the Open University

If you have not already enrolled on the course and would like to purchase this or other Open University material, contact Open University Worldwide Ltd, The Berrill Building, Walton Hall, Milton Keynes MK7 6AA, United Kingdom: tel. +44 (0)1908 858785; fax +44 (0)1908 858787; email ouwenq@open.ac.uk; website http://www.ouw.co.uk

1.1

Contents

Theme Introductions

Sustainability is one of the five Themes you will cover while studying this course. The other four Themes are: *Transitions, Poverty and Inequality, Technology and Knowledge, Displacement.*

Five weeks of study are set aside during Part 1 of U213 for these Theme Introductions, each comprising one week. You are expected to study them after you have completed your study of *Poverty and Development into the 21st Century* (Allen and Thomas, 2000; hereafter called the Course Book) and its associated audiocassettes, as directed by *Study Guide 1*. At the end of this five-week period a further week is set aside for you to complete tutor-marked assignment TMA 03 and to make your Theme choices for Part 2 of the course.

Remember that in Part 2 you will study *three* of the five Themes in the following order:

> *Transitions* (compulsory Theme)
>
> *Poverty and Inequality* or *Technology and Knowledge*
>
> *Displacement* or *Sustainability.*

The final section of *Study Guide 1* provides information that should help you make your choices. You should return to this once you have completed your study of the Theme Introductions.

Even if you are already certain which Themes you intend to study in Part 2 you should study all five Introductions in Part 1, including this one. This is because each Introduction practises skills that are relevant to other Themes and, also, we expect you to obtain a rounded view before you specialize. You may be assessed in your final examination on the learning outcomes associated with any of the Introductions. You will also be encouraged to illustrate TMA 03 with examples from a range of the Themes.

The Theme Introductions are self-contained, although they all assume that you have completed your study of the Course Book and its associated audiocassettes. We recommend, however, that you study them during this five-week period in the following order:

First week	*Transitions*
Second week	*Poverty and Inequality*
Third week	*Technology and Knowledge*
Fourth week	*Displacement*
Fifth week	*Sustainability*

The sixth week has been set aside for completing TMA 03 and making your choices for Part 2 of the course.

Studying *Introduction to Sustainability*

Some general aims of this Introduction are presented below. We also provide a checklist of learning outcomes. These are what we expect you to be able to do once you have completed the Introduction and are what you are potentially assessed upon in your TMAs and/or final examination.

The main text contains activities for you to undertake. These are included to engage you *actively* with the text and to foster deeper level study than you will be able to achieve simply by reading. Typically these activities check that you understand what is being written and can critically engage with it, and draw you into the process of developing the text argument. Do therefore attempt to do the activities before reading the comments that follow them. The main text also directs you from time to time to the Course Book, so make sure that you always have this to hand.

You should aim to complete studying this text in one week (about 12–14 hours of study time) which means that you should think of ways to divide up your time to work through this material. This will naturally vary between students depending on when you have time available to work and how quickly you can go through the material.

Aims and skills

This Introduction helps you to understand how to:
- explore different uses of the terms 'sustainability' and 'sustainable development', their common characteristics, and how they inter-relate;
- explore the possibilities for active and conscious management of development processes in order to work towards sustainable development.

It also develops the following skills:
- Conceptual skills to help you analyse key issues and arguments concerning sustainability and sustainable development.
- Mapping skills to use as tools to help you find your way around the complexity of sustainability and sustainable development debates.
- Numerical skills in the use of indices that attempt to capture some of the complexities of sustainability and sustainable development in quantitative data.

These skills are only developed to an introductory level in this text. They, and other skills, will be developed further in Part 2 of the *Sustainability* Theme.

Learning outcomes

After studying this *Introduction to Sustainability* you should be able to do the following:

1   Identify different dimensions of sustainability and their common characteristics of continuity over time, robustness, and effectiveness.

2   Apply these common characteristics as basic criteria for assessing progress towards sustainability of a development intervention and understand the difficulties associated with such an application.

3   Use simple mapping techniques to navigate the complexity of sustainability issues.

4   Understand the use of indices for capturing the multiple dimensions of sustainability.

5   Articulate the relationship between sustainability and sustainable development.

6   Appreciate the general importance of civil society in holding powerful actors to account with respect to sustainability and sustainable development.

7   Analyse critically the World Commission on Environment and Development (WCED) 'standard' definition of sustainable development, especially its conceptualization in terms of 'needs'.

8   Understand that sustainability and sustainable development require active management towards defined goals; also the importance of accountability and learning processes to active management.

9   Understand the importance for sustainability and sustainable development of actively managing both broad processes (such as industrialization and globalization) and deliberate development actions.

10 Recognize the importance of livelihoods, institutions, technologies and physical resource use in sustainability and sustainable development debates.

11 Understand and apply to a limited number of examples a framework for assessing the contribution of given development actions to sustainability and sustainable development.

1 The subject of this Theme

Sustainability is one of those words that 'took off' during the last decades of the twentieth century, especially in relation to areas connected to development. Thus, it is not uncommon today to hear it used to refer to the sustainability of national economic policies, of political systems, of public services such as health, education and waste management, of ways of life (or 'cultures'), of an inanimate physical resource such as oil, and so on. We even refer to the 'sustainability of development', although we generally use a short-hand form of these words – *sustainable development*. Within 'deliberate' development (see the Course Book, Chapter 2), agencies are invariably concerned with the sustainability of projects that they help set up.

What, however, do we mean by the term *sustainability*? One thing to note from today's myriad uses of the term is that sustainability has no meaning except in relation to something else. Thus we should always refer to the sustainability *of* something (as in the sustainability of a biological species – see below) or use it as an adjective (as in sustainable development). One of the aims of this text is to explore some of these different uses in relation to development, to draw out their common characteristics, and to explore how they might inter-relate.

> Historically, the term *sustainability* was applied to the harvesting of a specific renewable species, such as a particular species of fish in a fishery or a particular type of tree in a forest … Subsequently to this usage, ecologists adopted the term to refer to the status and function of ecological systems, such as the Amazon rain forest.
>
> (Weaver *et al.*, 1997, pp.238, 239)

This first application of sustainability described in the above quotation is relatively straightforward to understand and is best illustrated by an example. Thus, if the harvesting (catch) rate of cod in the Atlantic Ocean exceeds the growth rate of the stock of cod, eventually the cod will be fished into extinction.

The subsequent application, while still rooted in biology, was invoked to deal with the complexity surrounding the sustainability of an ecosystem, as opposed to that of a single species. In order to do this, the concept of *carrying capacity* was introduced. Carrying capacity is the ability of an ecosystem* to absorb and process external disturbance, such as depletion of one or more of its various components or degradation from pollutants. In terms of a forest, this might mean the ability to regenerate trees that have been felled in logging operations and/or the ability to withstand, say, pollution from acid rain downwind of an electricity-generating power station.

*Ecosystem: a community of organisms, interacting with one another, plus the environment in which they live and with which they also interact.

Arising from these historical roots, sustainability has been strongly associated with conservation – not taking from Earth, from society, from each other more than we can give back (Rahnema, p.380). Rahnema goes on to claim, however, that this association has become corrupted to rationalizing the conservation of injustice in the world. Thus, as stated above, we have to ask ourselves: 'Sustainability of what?' The answer is not always benign, something else we explore in this text.

The association with conservation informed the early international concerns over sustainability in relation to global development, when, in 1972, 'The Club of Rome' (Box 1.1) published its then influential *The Limits to Growth* (Meadows *et al.*, 1972). The basic argument in this publication was that economic growth was using up the Earth's natural resources at an unprecedented rate, some of which, if the rate of depletion continued unchecked, would be exhausted within a single human lifetime (or even less in some cases).

Meadows *et al.* themselves returned to the fray in 1992 with the publication of *Beyond the Limits* as a sequel to their original book and which argued that many resource and pollution flows had grown beyond sustainable limits (Meadows *et al.*, 1992).

The unambiguous conclusion from this assessment of the situation (and implied by the book's title) was that conservation of the Earth's resources and unbridled economic growth are ultimately incompatible. Given that, at that time (and despite the advocacy in some quarters of the basic needs approach) mainstream thinking associated development principally with economic growth, it was not hard to extend the 'Limits to growth' argument to development itself. Understandably, developing countries bridled against it, asserting their 'right to development' alongside the 'already developed' countries, an argument that was still running strong 20 years later at the first United Nations Conference on Environment and Development (UNCED) – the so-called Earth Summit held in Rio de Janeiro, 1992.

Before UNCED, however, a United Nations Commission, the World Commission on Environment and Development (WCED) which was chaired by the Norwegian prime minister, Gro Harlem Brundtland (hence its colloquial name, the Brundtland Commission), had begun the task of grappling with the issue of reconciling environmental sustainability and 'the right to development'. The outcome was another influential book, *Our Common Future*, and the oft-quoted definition of sustainable development as:

> ... development that meets the needs of the present without compromising the ability of future generations to meet their own needs.
>
> (Brundtland, 1987)

Over the years since *Our Common Future* was published, this definition has received rigorous scrutiny and refinement, and you will find that this text engages with some of the debates that it has engendered. Most of these are based on the observation that the definition, by itself, ignores *spatial equity*. Thus although the definition is concerned with conserving for future generations (and hence does show a concern for *inter-generational equity*), it ignores current (and future) divisions in the world between, for example, rich and poor countries. This has led writers such as Wolfgang Sachs (among others) to accuse the WCED of

Box 1.1 The Club of Rome

The Club of Rome is an organization set up in 1968 by an international group of industrialists, economists, scientists, politicians and others. The club was founded on the initiative of an Italian business executive and developed from umbrella organizations founded to represent the interests of large companies in Europe which were at least partly owned by foreign interests (Pepper, 1984).

One of the most influential publications sponsored by the Club of Rome was *The Limits to Growth* by D. Meadows *et al.*, published in 1972. This report examined the trends, at that time, in world population, industrialization, pollution, food production and resource depletion. The authors used computer modelling to extrapolate from these trends and predict the future of human society. As with all users of modelling techniques they made various assumptions on which to base their model. Their prediction was that the Earth's limits to growth would be reached within decades. Limited resources and increased pollution would result in a sudden and catastrophic decline in population due to a rising death rate from lack of food and pollution. The authors also ran their model using various alternative assumptions of change in future policy such as full use of resources, greatly increased recycling rates, pollution reduction and effective birth control. These measures could delay the crisis but to avoid catastrophe all together would, among other factors, require an abandonment of economic growth as an overall world policy. Despite the gloomy forecast from the model, the report postulated that it would be possible to avoid catastrophe by introducing policies designed to achieve economic and ecological stability that would be sustainable into the distant future. The report met severe criticism on several grounds. In particular, the assumptions made and conditions applied in the computer model were called into question. However, despite its shortcomings, *The Limits to Growth* raised awareness of resource depletion, economic stability and environmental degradation in international politics and significantly influenced policies at the time.

Golub and Townsend (1977) took a cynical view of the whole study – or at least of the way in which selected aspects of it had been emphasized by the Club of Rome. They had, it was maintained, hoped to create a climate of despondency and foreboding in which people would be willing to sacrifice national aspirations for the 'greater global good'. This would mean greater acceptance of the notion of international bodies exerting control over national economies – and within such a framework the multinational corporations which were represented by the Club of Rome would be freer to act in their own interests, unfettered by nationally imposed constraints on their freedom.

ultimately siding with nature and not justice (Sachs, p.294). Again, this was a major source of debate between rich and poorer countries at the aforementioned Earth Summit, with the latter essentially demanding that:

- the rich countries should bear the cost of clearing up the environmental mess because it was they that created it, and continue to contribute to it in large share, by their past industrialization;

- linked to the poorer countries' right to development, the rich countries should provide the means by which the former can engage economically in environment-conserving industrialization by, for example, making available on concessionary terms new technologies that address environmental concerns.

The debates and demands are still with us, but it is important not to become too polarized by them. Today they are wrapped within a broader agenda of how to *manage* development in a broad-based (paying attention to 'spatial equity') and sustainable way. Today's debates have moved on, therefore, in that they are about ways of *operationalizing* sustainable development (i.e. making it happen). Although another criticism of the WCED (Brundtland) definition above is that it does not indicate *how* sustainable development might be achieved, the idea flows from it that management in a broad sense is necessary, in that the definition provides a vision which we should try to find ways of realizing.

The idea of sustainable development as management is a major concern of this Introduction. Firstly, in Section 2, the different contexts in which the term sustainability is used are explored and a more holistic approach is suggested that recognizes the inter-relationships of the different contexts. Then Section 3 establishes some broad criteria that we might use to assess progress towards sustainability whatever the context, followed by Section 4 which examines mechanisms by which sustainability might be achieved. Finally, Section 5 draws the three previous sections together in a discussion of sustainable development as active management.

2 Sustainability in context

But development must be sustainable. It is the Earth's natural resources that fulfil our basic needs. There can be no lasting development if we rob from the future to pay our bills for today. This is why the UK Department for International Development (DFID) has made wise management of the environment a cornerstone of its development policy.

(DFID, 1998)

There are plenty of examples of heavily funded Government-sponsored Programmes that run for [up to] seven years, but when the money runs out the whole thing runs to a terrible halt and people are almost left in a worse position than they were before ... we can either pay an organization to fund community workers, and then we have to say what happens when the money runs out, or we can pay to support existing organizations who are involved in community development work and work with them on the basis that they will still be here when the money runs out. That's what the Board [of a participatory development programme in the UK] understands by sustainability.

(Wilson, 2000, p.295)

All the community want is to have a say in what goes on ... and to take ownership, because at the end of the day that's sustainability.

(Wilson, 2000, p.295)

When industrial society uses the word [sustainability], it means the sustaining of itself, no matter what the cost. It means sustaining privilege, sustaining poverty, sustaining abuse of the earth, sustaining inequality, sustaining starvation, sustaining violence.

(Rahnema, 1997, p.380)

Many things are tied up with the words 'sustainability' and 'sustainable development', as the above small selection of quotations shows. It is this proliferation of emphases, interpretations and meanings that lead some to see in the terms the possibility of an idea that unites people on Earth under a common banner ('We all want sustainability and sustainable development, don't we?'), while for others the proliferation renders the terms meaningless, with any attempt to forge common, united action out of them doomed.

Activity 1

Examine more closely the quotations above and also the WCED (Brundtland) definition of sustainable development in Section 1. Complete the table below which suggests possible contexts (the 'environmental sustainability' context, etc.) in which the terms 'sustainability' or 'sustainable' are being used. For each quotation you should place two ticks in the appropriate cell for what you consider to be the main context in which the terms are used; and one tick for what you consider to be other contexts that are at least implied by the quotation. Leave cells blank if you feel particular contexts are not addressed. Don't worry if you do not have a very precise sense of what the different

11

contexts are, because that is not the point of the exercise, and broad 'common sense' understandings will suffice. I have completed the cells for the UK Department of International Development (DFID) as an example of what is required.

Quotation	Environmental sustainability	Economic sustainability	Social sustainability	Political sustainability
Brundtland				
DFID	√√	√	√	
Wilson 1				
Wilson 2				
Rahnema				

Comment

I am going to deal with the WCED (Brundtland) quotation last because I think it is the most difficult on which to do this box-filling exercise. But, taking the others in the order in which they appear:

The DFID quotation clearly highlights the environment, but its reference to (deferred) payment suggests an economic angle. Also it is used alongside the word 'development'. This term, as you know from your study of the first 10 weeks of the course, also has a multiplicity of meanings, but I assume that DFID intends development to have a social (as is also implied by the quotation's use of another term from the Course Book, 'basic needs') as well as an economic dimension. Thus, there is a social angle to sustainability in this quotation too.

The two statements about sustainability in Wilson (2000) have been made by different people, although they concern the same development intervention – regeneration of a deprived community in the city of Bradford, UK.

The first Wilson quotation highlights the economic sustainability issues concerning development interventions. 'What is going to happen when the funding ends?', is a common question asked of all interventions. The quotation does also specify social development interventions and thus implies social sustainability.

The second Wilson quotation is rather different. It suggests that sustainability concerns local people having control and a sense of ownership of development interventions that are done in their name. Who decides who gets what, is, broadly speaking, the stuff of politics. Hence, I think that this quotation has a strong political sustainability component.

The Rahnema quotation raises a whole bundle of issues, all of a socio-economic nature, apart from 'sustaining abuse of the Earth' which is more obviously environmental. There are again, in the quotation, overtones of who decides who gets what (industrial society doesn't decide; certain people within industrial society do) so there is also an implied political sustainability dimension.

We finally arrive at the 'classic' definition of sustainable development formulated by the WCED (Brundtland). Taken as a stark quotation, it seems to relate to everything and nothing at the same time. It is about environmental sustainability as the title of the Commission indicates. It's also about justice, which links it to the Rahnema quotation, but as Section 1 indicates, justice of a particular kind – justice for future generations. It says nothing about the composition of those generations (whether present or future) and whether within them privilege, poverty and inequality may be sustained. Perhaps these issues are covered by the word 'development', but again we know from the Course Book that this need not be the case. In other words, the quotation begs the issue of 'Whose sustainable development?' and, in particular whether it is possible to have sustainable development for some and not for others. Thus the problem with the WCED definition of sustainable development (and a problem for all definitions that attempt to be all-encompassing) is that it leaves too much open to interpretation.

Let me finish this comment on the first activity by showing you my completed table:

Quotation	Environmental sustainability	Economic sustainability	Social sustainability	Political sustainability
WCED	√	√	√	√
DFID	√√	√	√	
Wilson 1		√√	√	
Wilson 2				√√
Rahnema	√√	√√	√√	√

Even if you disagree with the precise allocation of ticks in the above completed table, you should have discovered from Activity 1 that sustainability is used in many contexts. This flows from the point made in Section 1 that sustainability is always in relation to something. And that 'something' can be very varied as even a casual glance at several of the chapters in the Course Book will show.

For example, to take the section 'A world of problems?' from the Course Book, sustainability contexts and associated questions that either derive directly from a chapter's stated questions or its main arguments might be:

Chapter 3: the context of *food*. How can livelihoods, or entitlements, be created and sustained in order to prevent famine?

Chapter 4: the context of *health*. (a) How can interventions provide sustainable improvements in health? (b) Is the toll of HIV/AIDS making whole societies in some parts of the world unsustainable?

Chapter 5: the context of *work*. (a) Are employment opportunities in low-income countries sufficient to provide sustainable livelihoods? (b) In what ways does diversity of ways of making a living help sustain livelihoods in these countries?

Chapter 6: the context of *population growth*. (a) Is global population growth unsustainable? And relatedly (b) Can new thinking on population interventions be translated into sustainable action?

Chapter 7: the *environmental* context again. (a) In what ways can people's livelihoods also become environmentally sustainable? (b) How can development be made (environmentally) sustainable?

Chapter 8: the context of *war*. Is contemporary war sustainable?

As suggested above, this ability to use sustainability in almost any development context is both the concept's strength and its weakness: its strength because it provides a possible common 'big idea' behind almost all development activity that can unite diverse perspectives, whatever the specific nature of that activity; its weakness because it comes to mean all things to all people (or, as the summary of Chapter 21 says about culture: it 'explains everything and nothing in particular' (p.466)).

Now look again at the two Wilson quotations near the beginning of this section. The first is about whether to pay for community workers directly out of the intervention's money or to support existing organizations involved in community work. It inclines towards the latter, suggesting that sustainability is less about creating new institutions for social development (which can only be funded by the intervention for a limited period) and more about using the intervention to strengthen existing ones. So it argues that sustainability of social development interventions is about embedding them in existing organizations that share similar institutional values and practices (Box 2.1). The second Wilson quotation, in contrast, is about establishing new institutional practices of decision-making, where the community that is the subject of the social development interventions has ownership of what goes on.

Box 2.1 Institutions

Institutions concern mutually accepted values and ways of doing things within a defined population. These values and ways of doing things may be embodied in formal organizational structures, such as:

- The institution of Government, which is supposed to embody the values and ways of doing things of the people under its jurisdiction.
- The Open University with its commitment to Open Learning and a set of practices associated with that.

But institutions don't have to be synonymous with large organizations. Consider, for example:

- The institution of marriage, which embodies certain values and the practices of, at most, very informal organizations.
- Markets, which mean certain norms and practices of 'doing business'. They may link individual buyers and sellers, or they may link organizations (such as companies in trading relationships), but by themselves markets are not organizations.

These examples have been described as if they are 'ideal' types, but governments often do not embody the values and ways of doing things of many of the people under their jurisdiction. Such governments may even be said, in more extreme circumstances, to lack legitimacy in the eyes of most of their population. Also, markets invariably depart from their 'ideal' types – indeed, *Introduction to Transitions* establishes that markets are 'made' and, rather than representing some abstract 'ideal', they are better described as *social* (i.e. socially constructed) institutions.

We will return to the institutional context of sustainability later in the text, but I want to end this section by pointing out that many current ideas about sustainability are 'holistic' – they combine various dimensions of sustainability in different ways. The following is an example from the UK Department for International Development (DFID) which has placed the concept of 'sustainable livelihoods' at the centre of its anti-poverty, international aid strategy. Again, a discussion of 'sustainable livelihoods' will appear later in the text, but consider what DFID has to say about sustainability within this context:

> [Sustainability] is the core concept without which development effort is wasted. Policies to reduce poverty, whether the actual interventions are at local or national level, must be sustainable and continue to achieve their objectives. Sustainability, in the context of livelihoods approaches, includes not only continuing poverty reduction but, among others, environmental, social and institutional sustainability. Crucial to the success and sustainability of all interventions is the concept of good governance. Policies and services should not exclude the poor, they should meet the needs of the people and they must be properly managed and regulated at all levels.
>
> (DFID, 2000)

Activity 2

Within an overall 'context of sustainable livelihoods', the DFID quotation suggests several other contexts. List them.

Comment

Environmental, social and institutional sustainabilities are explicitly mentioned in the quotation. They have also been highlighted as contexts of sustainability in the discussion above. You will have come across the concept of 'governance' before, in *Study Guide 1*. In this context it is referring to the development and management of policy on poverty and recognizes that this is not the province of a single player, such as a country's government (if it was we would use 'government' rather than 'governance') or an international aid agency. The quotation also can be interpreted to suggest that 'the poor' should be part of governance structures and echoes the second Wilson quotation at the start of the section. It is roughly equivalent to what we have termed 'political sustainability' in the previous comment.

The quotation goes even further than these contexts, however, and refers to the sustainability of poverty reduction. The implication is that such sustainability is dependent on the other contexts, and thus is of a different order to them. But the reference to sustainable poverty reduction does suggest that 'sustainability' is not value free, something else that we flag here for later in the text.

We have muddied the waters a fair bit in the few pages of this Introduction that you have studied so far. We have highlighted several different contexts of sustainability and hinted that there are many more, We have also suggested that these contexts might be better combined to give us a more holistic view of sustainability. But we need to draw out some core, common criteria for examining the different contexts; otherwise sustainability does become meaningless as a unifying concept. It is to these that we now turn.

Summary of Section 2

1 Sustainability has many contexts in which it is used: for example, the environmental, economic, social and political contexts. 'Sustainable livelihoods' is another context that is currently favoured by several international aid agencies.

2 Contemporary views of sustainability tend to view it more holistically in a number of inter-related contexts at once.

3 Criteria for assessing sustainability

This section explores ideas of continuity, robustness and effectiveness as criteria for assessing sustainability, whatever the context in which the term is used.

3.1 Continuity and robustness

The WCED (Brundtland, 1987) quotation in Section 1 and the DFID (1998) and DFID (2000) quotations in Section 2 all refer to sustaining the present or today into the future, which we call *continuity over time*. The first Wilson quotation at the start of Section 2 is a bit more specific – what happens when the money runs out in seven years' time? How is this project going to sustain itself then?

The first Wilson quotation also introduces a feature that is related to continuity over time, when it refers to supporting 'existing organizations who are involved in community development work and work with them on the basis that they will still be here when the money runs out' – that of *robustness*. In this instance it is implied that established organizations tend to be robust in that they keep on going and are less vulnerable to 'shocks' such as withdrawal by the funding agency that provided the initial injection of resource.

More generally, robustness includes being able to secure access to the input resources that are needed for continuing (and developing) an activity. Such inputs may be any combination of financial, human (people and their skills) and 'natural' resources.* Access to these input resources may be secured by generating from within the activity one kind of resource which may then be used to procure the other necessary inputs that cannot be generated from within. The common example is that of a private firm that generates financial resources from the sale of the goods and services it produces to procure human (i.e. labour) and physical inputs for its continuing operations. In development interventions, what are often known as income-generation projects, set up to help poor people secure a living, are conceived by their sponsoring aid agencies in these terms. After a relatively short period of funding, the projects are expected to be able to generate financial resources from within themselves, which they use to gain access to the other resources they need.

*There is an issue over the use of 'natural' with its implication that some resources exist independently of humans and their influence. For the purposes of this text we need not enter this debate and a common-sense understanding is sufficient here. In Box 3.1 below and later sections, however, we will distinguish between physical, biological and environmental 'natural' resources.

Robustness of an activity whose aim is to generate income is fairly easy to understand. The difficulty arises when the activity is to perform some kind of public service – such as education and health – where at most only a fraction of the cost of providing it can be recovered from the users of the service. In these cases, access to the necessary input resources can only be secured if one has institutional rights to them. Thus a government may obtain the financial resources for running a health or education service from taxation of the population, which can then be used to procure the other resources that are required. An established charity that performs a social service may obtain its resources through direct appeals to the public; it may also receive some funds directly from government. Charities (and governments), in practice, will often try to diversify their sources of (usually financial) resources so that they do not become overly dependent on only one.

The related concerns of continuity over time and robustness in relation to social and economic development activity have a history that goes back at least to the 1970s. Consider the following 'snapshots' of income-generation projects recorded in an Oxfam handbook published in 1990.

> In Ahmedabad, India, a [workers' co-operative] was established with the support of a local NGO [non-government organization]. This support has continued with varying intensity for almost ten years. The NGO's project officer with responsibility for the co-op spends most of her time working with them, trying to arrange market outlets, helping to develop and maintain a book-keeping and accounts system, assisting with management decisions and looking for funders. The substantial costs of the project officer's time and overheads are borne by the NGO and constitute a considerable subsidy to the co-op.
>
> (Hurley, 1990, p.50)

> In North East Brazil a women's co-operative producing woven rugs was initiated by a middle class woman. The aim was to use the waste material from a textile factory some miles from the participants' homes, but neither the interveners nor the participants had much, if any, business experience. The objectives of the project were strongly imbued with the aim of women's empowerment.
>
> After several years of basic business problems – low sales, stockpiling, high costs, considerable need for subsidies – the enterprise was far from becoming economically viable. Particular problems arose from inadequate management by 'expert' outsiders who did not take the necessary steps to prepare themselves to offer useful support to the economic side of the venture, and who, after considerable initial efforts became discouraged by continuing economic failure. Funding for the project may now no longer be available from the donor aid agency and the relationship between the interveners and the participants has soured...
>
> (Hurley, 1990, p.60)

Activity 3

In what ways do these snapshots illustrate issues of continuity over time and robustness?

Comment

The tone of the above snapshots suggests that neither of these development interventions can be described as unqualified successes! The reasons are to do with the continuing financial burden placed on the donor agency in each case and an implied concern that the projects may collapse once the donors withdraw. Also implied is a more general unease with dependency on outside financial support and expertise (Figure 3.1).

Figure 3.1 A Voluntary Service Overseas worker talking to women in Sudan.

In the language of the 1990s, if an activity was not robust, it was because it was 'vulnerable' which in turn was because it was 'dependent' in some way.

Dependency concerns tended to dominate discussion of the effectiveness of aid during the 1990s. Dependency was considered to be a particularly deviant and malignant tendency in the dominant neoliberal discourse of the time, and continues to have reverberations during the early 2000s. In colloquial terms the argument runs as follows: people and nations should be encouraged to 'stand on their own two feet', 'take personal responsibility for their lives', and that is 'the way out of poverty'.

Do you recognize these arguments about 'standing on one's own two feet' and 'taking personal responsibility' from your own country? Can you think of examples?

Oxfam was one of the early aid agencies to try to grapple with these concerns using the concept of sustainability. Thus, in 1990, it said of income-generation projects:

> There is continuing debate in development circles about the sustainability of aid and on how long donors can or should sustain their subsidies or funding for programmes. The emphasis here is on the different, but linked question of the sustainability, i.e. continuing viability, of an economic activity. A central aim of an intervention that has prioritized income generation in its objectives should be that the economic activity will eventually be able to survive completely independently of aid or subsidy in any form. Otherwise the intervention will remain a welfare handout, leaving the participants dependent on the interveners and vulnerable to the cessation of aid. This undermines them both economically and socially.
>
> (Hurley, 1990, p.50)

Note in this quotation again the concern of dependency (and vulnerability, which is more directly the antithesis of robustness) in relation to what happens when aid is withdrawn. The tone, as encapsulated by the last sentence, however, is not so much about the neoliberal discourse of encouraging people 'to stand on their own two feet' as about empowerment, or specifically here its opposite, disempowerment.

Activity 4

Turn to the discussion of empowerment on pages 34 and 35 of the Course Book. In what way does it suggest that empowerment involves rather more than encouraging 'people to stand on their own two feet'.

Comment

Clearly, being able to 'stand on one's own two feet' is an element of empowerment if people are to take 'direct control over their lives' and be 'agents of their own development', and neoliberal commentators will emphasize precisely this aspect when they use the term 'empowerment'. The discussion on page 35 of the Course Book, however, also stresses that this is not possible for most people without 'changes in power structures both at local and at broader, national and international levels ... Empowerment, then, implies redistributing power and transforming institutions.'

This discussion reveals again the widely differing standpoints from which sustainability (and empowerment for that matter) is approached. It is no surprise, therefore, that people using the concept might be meaning quite different things, and a first job of any discussion of sustainability is to disentangle these different meanings.

The above quotations from Oxfam illustrate well how the international aid community has come to emphasize a particular meaning of sustainability. This community is driven by a particular agenda – the effectiveness of its aid programmes in meeting their objectives, and how efficiently its resources are used in these programmes: hence the concerns over dependency and what happens once funding ceases. A recipient of the aid may, however, be less concerned with the sustainability of specific donor-funded programmes – where the recipient may have little control over the resources that are being provided – than the contribution that these projects and programmes make to the sustainability of, say, a whole sector (such as education or health) or to more general aspects of life. Thus an article on sustainability which used the example of the health sector in Ghana commented:

> ...the donors' notion of sustainability is at least one step removed from the sustainability problem that countries themselves are facing. Donors pay more attention to the life of the project than to the contribution that project might be making to health system development. Evidence suggests, however, that the persistent demise of externally financed activities is just a symptom of a deeper sustainability dilemma facing health systems throughout the developing world. Despite 14 years of investment in PHC [primary health care], health systems in low income countries continue to suffer from misallocation of resources, inequity,

inefficiency and exploding costs. The search for the key to 'project donor sustainability' must therefore yield to a more important question: how best to ensure the sustainability of the entire health system?

(LaFond, 1995, p.29)

The examples I have used above to illustrate continuity over time and robustness, and their mirror images of withdrawal of funding and vulnerability or dependency, have been in terms of economic and social sustainability. Look again at these examples and you will see too that the issues have generally been about the continuing availability of, and control over, financial or human resources or both.

We can also apply the same criteria, or variants of them, to other contexts, such as physical resource sustainability. Here, the continuity issue relates to being able to continue to make available the physical resource (for example by finding fresh deposits) or to carry on once it is depleted or so degraded that it is of no further value (for example by using substitute resources) (Box 3.1). The robustness issue is relatedly about not being dependent on inputs of a particular physical resource for an activity or activities. For example, many argue that countries are too dependent on oil for their energy needs, which makes them vulnerable to adverse changes in access to the resource. This is why, moreover, there are so many disputes related to oil – from international wars over access to the resource, to the 'people's' fuel tax revolt that swept through Western Europe during 2000 (Figure 3.2).

Figure 3.2 Taxi drivers block traffic on the highway out of Charles de Gaulle airport in Roissy, north of Paris, 7 September 2000. Taxi drivers joined truckers and farmers in their protest against rising fuel prices.

Box 3.1 Physical resources and their exploitation

Resources is a word applied in many different contexts. A general definition is the means of supplying what is needed. Most basic human needs for food, shelter and so on can be met from the Earth's natural resources. Natural resources can be further divided into biological (plants, animals) and physical (rocks, fossil fuels, mineral ores, water) resources. There are also less tangible natural resources such as living space, land, and the air around us: these are sometimes called environmental resources.

Rocks, fossil fuels and minerals are all examples of non-renewable resources. The processes that formed them took place over many millions of years of the Earth's history. They are in finite supply and if we continue to exploit them, ultimately there will come a time when the resources will run out. Forecasting when that might be is not an easy task and depends on many varying factors, notably the rate at which we exploit the resource and the reserves that exist. *Reserves* are those parts of a resource which have been proven to exist, by survey for example, and are recoverable, by mining or some other method of extraction. They are deemed *usable reserves* only if it is economically sensible and technically feasible to extract them. The amount of usable reserves of any physical resource is therefore not a fixed quantity – it will depend on developments in extraction techniques and on the changing economic value of the end product.

For physical resources, the first stage in the transformation from raw material to end product is extraction from the Earth, usually by mining or quarrying. Coal for energy production, stone and rock for construction and ores for metal production all come out of holes in the ground.

In their natural state, metals are almost always found, not as nuggets of pure metal, but as chemical compounds within the rock. For any rock to be classified as an ore, it must contain sufficient quantities of these compounds to be separated economically. Metals are a relatively high-value product so even very small quantities are worth extracting. The proportion of metal in an ore is typically very small; even the highest grade ores contain large quantities of waste material that is simply discarded when the ore is processed. Figure 3.3 shows the relative proportions of ore, ore concentrate and refined metal.

The relative proportion of waste to end product is huge and the resulting spoil heaps are one of the most significant environmental impacts of mineral exploitation. The waste dumps at Bingham Canyon copper mine in Utah, USA, the biggest copper mine in the world, are visible from 20 km away.

Sustainability of physical resources exploitation is, therefore, not only a question of non-renewability and the assessment of reserves – the effects of the exploitation on the environment are equally important. Long before the limited reserves of a resource become a problem, its continued extraction can become unsustainable because of the related impacts.

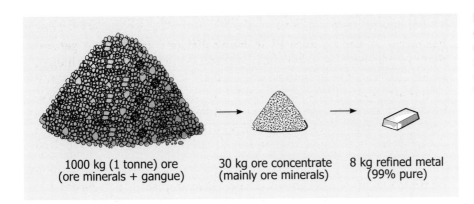

1000 kg (1 tonne) ore
(ore minerals + gangue)

30 kg ore concentrate
(mainly ore minerals)

8 kg refined metal
(99% pure)

3.2 Effectiveness

I want to return in this subsection to the DFID (2000) quotation that appeared just before Activity 2 in Section 2. In the comment that followed that activity I suggested that the DFID concern with poverty reduction indicates that sustainability is not value free. The comment above about empowerment meaning different things to neoliberals and a development NGO such as Oxfam also reinforces this point.

The DFID quotation raises two basic questions:

1   What is to be sustained?

2   For whom is it to be sustained?

Activity 5

Examine the DFID (2000) quotation just before Activity 2 again and try to answer the above questions in relation to it before reading on.

Comment

I think the answers are fairly clear. 'Policies to reduce poverty' must be sustained; and these policies are primarily for 'the poor' (although you might argue that they're also for DFID and other international aid donors).

To push these answers further, what kinds of policy are we talking about? A policy to reduce poverty might be *effective* in achieving that aim in the short term and may represent an *efficient* use of funds (Box 3.2), but might equally be very difficult to sustain over time. In contrast, another policy might be less effective in achieving poverty reduction even in the short term, but is easier to sustain over time. LaFond, quoted earlier with respect to health services in Ghana, makes the same point when she says:

> The perpetuation of a health system which fails to meet health needs is of little value ... a sustainable system must function *effectively* [emphasis in the original] over time...

(LaFond, 1995, p.30)

Once we start talking about effective development activities we enter again territory that is certain to be contested. *Effectiveness* is about how successful one is in achieving stated goals, so the first dispute might be about what those goals are. But even if, for example, it is accepted that the stated goal is reducing poverty, disputes will continue to arise, for how we examine success in that endeavour depends on how we conceptualize poverty in the first place. Your work on the Course Book and on *Introduction to Poverty and Inequality* should have made it clear that poverty can be thought of in a myriad ways – from lack of income to broader, multi-dimensional views – and each conceptualization will rely on different indicators to measure progress (or lack of it).

If you are unclear about these different conceptualizations of poverty, turn to the Course Book, Chapter 1, Section 1.2 and/or *Introduction to Poverty and Inequality*, Section 3.

Box 3.2 Effectiveness and efficiency

These two terms are often used interchangeably, but they are not the same. As the text states, effectiveness is about how successful one is in achieving stated goals. Efficiency, however, is the ratio of output from an activity to input; e.g. the number of children who may be immunized in a health campaign per dollar of input.

If the stated goal of an activity concerns efficiency, such as immunizing the greatest number of children for the least cost, then effectiveness and efficiency are essentially the same. If, however, the stated aim is improving the physical health of the community, this may have to be judged in relation to other, broader criteria. For example, it may be found that efficient immunization only has a marginal effect on physical health because, for example, diarrhoea (for which there is no vaccine) is the main scourge.

Activity 6

Assume for the moment that you hold a multi-dimensional view of poverty. How would you assess the likely effectiveness of a development project designed to provide income-generating opportunities for poor women?

Comment

This is an interesting question because you are asked to assess from a multi-dimensional perspective an intervention that is designed to address directly one dimension of poverty – that of lack of income (Figure 3.4). Even if it was shown to be successful in increasing the income of poor women I would want to know about the intervention's possible knock-on effects (both positive and negative) on other dimensions of poverty. For example, the women might be doing this income-generation activity in addition to the other tasks that they already perform, and their health suffers through overwork (a negative impact on this dimension of poverty). In contrast, earning more money may

Figure 3.4 Women in Bangladesh embroidering articles for sale.

Figure 3.5 Afforestation programme taking place in Scotland.

mean that the women are able to feed themselves better, which, other things being equal, would be a positive impact on their health. Earning an independent income might also have positive gender-related impacts, such as greater independence from husbands. Clearly, we would need to understand the full context in which this income-generating project is conceived in order to assess its effectiveness from a multi-dimensional perspective on poverty, but the point is that uni-dimensional development interventions can have multi-dimensional effects. If the context is correctly understood, it is possible for such interventions to be beneficial, therefore, just as the converse is also true – a multi-dimensional intervention on poverty might be ineffective because it tries to do everything at once and doesn't do any of it well.

Again we can relate this idea of effectiveness in social and economic development to environmental sustainability. Take, for example, an afforestation programme in an area that has suffered from indiscriminate logging (Figure 3.5). Planting quick-growing trees, all of the same species, might be effective in regenerating the forest cover (and an efficient way of doing it), but might not be effective in other ways. For example, the biodiversity of the area before deforestation would have depended on the unique mix of trees in the original forest, and this would be unlikely to return with a 'monoculture' of fast-growing trees. As a result, livelihood opportunities of local people who used to exploit the biodiversity of the original forest would still be limited (Box 3.3). Yet another possibility is that local people have been coerced into tree-planting in, say, a food-for-work programme and have consequently lost out on other livelihood opportunities.

Box 3.3 Biodiversity and livelihoods

Biodiversity, put simply, means the variety of all forms of life. It is usually taken to mean the diversity of species of living organisms, that is, all the plants, animals and other forms of life that exist on Earth. It also extends to include genetic diversity within species, known as the gene pool. On a wider scale it is often applied to the diversity of ecosystems. These encompass all the terrestrial and aquatic habitats on Earth including deciduous woodland, temperate grassland, tropical rainforest, deep ocean, shoreline, lake, desert and so on.

Although there are some uncertainties around the total number of species living in the world today, especially of plants and invertebrate animals, there is no doubt that many species are now extinct, or are threatened, as a result of human activities.

Major threats to biodiversity include:

1 Habitat loss and habitat fragmentation: demands on the land, exacerbated by increasing human population, contribute to loss of existing habitats in many ways including deforestation, urban development and intensive agriculture.

2 Over-exploitation: exemplified by the crash in commercial fish stocks in many parts of the world.

3 Exotic species: accidental or deliberate introduction of non-indigenous species can threaten the native flora and fauna, either by competing more successfully for the same resources or by direct predation.

4 Pollution and climate change.

In a forest, maintaining the diversity of tree species is essential to the continuing value of the forest, both as an ecosystem and as the basis for dependent human livelihoods. In ecological terms, a diverse mix of tree species will produce a richer, more stable environment for other plants and animals. Stability is derived from the multiplicity of links that can exist between the different plant and animal species – the living components of the ecosystem. If one or two links are broken, for example by disease in a particular tree species, then others are available as alternatives. So the loss of a species causes a minor disruption rather than an ecological disaster. In contrast, a plantation, where a single tree species grows in monoculture, cannot provide the same ecological diversity.

In a similar way, maintaining the species diversity can be essential to human beings whose livelihood is closely tied to the trees and their uses. Different species may be preferred for different uses such as construction timbers, charcoal-making, furniture, basket-making, firewood. By selecting different trees for different purposes, people can maximize the potential of the resources available to them. If diversity is reduced, people's options are reduced and consequently so are their chances of successfully maintaining their livelihood.

Tricky as the concept is, effectiveness has to take its place alongside continuity over time and robustness as a criterion for assessing sustainability. This is encapsulated in LaFond's definition of sustainability with respect to health systems (the italicized emphases are mine):

> The capacity of a health system to function *effectively over time* with a *minimum of external input.*
>
> (LaFond, 1995, p.29)

3.3 Assessing progress towards sustainability

The criteria of continuity over time, robustness, and effectiveness identified above provide us with a means of assessing, or measuring, progress towards achieving sustainability. But Activity 6 above has already illustrated the difficulties involved in applying a criterion such as effectiveness to a given situation. Let us illustrate these difficulties further with respect to all three criteria by working through a couple of examples. You will note also in the first example below that one cannot discuss a physical resource such as copper without reference to other contexts, such as the context in which it is used and the context of those people whose livelihoods depend on the resource. In other words, a more complex, 'holistic' approach is needed. To help you find your way around this complexity, I introduce some simple mapping techniques.

Applying the criteria: (a) the sustainability of a physical resource – copper

Copper is a metal of value to human beings because it:

- is reasonably stable chemically – it does not corrode and disintegrate that easily – although you may have noticed that public buildings with, say, copper-plated roofs start to corrode into a green dust;
- is malleable and can be beaten into shape quite easily – hence its use in pipes and as copper sheeting;
- conducts heat readily – which explains its use in car radiators, for example;
- is a good conductor of electricity – wherever there is electricity there are copper wires.

Copper exists in the Earth's crust in ores (Box 3.1), where it is chemically combined with other elements of differing chemical compositions – both other metals and non-metals. These ores are mined for their copper, but separating the pure copper from the rest of the ore is not a simple matter technically and is also expensive. Much depends on the actual percentage (or concentration) of copper that is bound up in the ore, but this has never been high in absolute terms and the amount in mined ores has steadily decreased over the past 100 years (up to 5% copper in a typical ore 100 years ago, but usually less than 1% today). The lower the grade of the ore (i.e. the lower the percentage of copper it contains), the more expensive the process of extracting the copper from it becomes (other things being equal).

Let us now attempt to apply our sustainability criteria of continuity over time, robustness and effectiveness.

In terms of *continuity over time*, there is argument over whether the resource of copper is running out, or at least over the rate at which it is running out. It is useful here to distinguish between a physical resource and its usable reserves (see also Box 3.1 above). A *physical resource* is what exists on Earth and is of potential value to human beings. A *usable reserve* is that part of the resource that can be extracted profitably in economic terms using the currently available technologies. A hundred years ago, extracting copper from a 1% ore would probably not have been considered profitable and only higher grade ores would have been considered as usable reserves. But the higher grade ores began to run out – this spurred technical innovations that made extraction from lower grade ores less expensive, and so they became usable reserves.

There is also a direct supply and demand aspect to the relationship between resources and usable reserves, which can make the relationship fluctuate over relatively short timescales. Moving away from copper for the moment, some of you studying this text will remember the coal miners' strike in the UK in the mid-1980s. The (official) heart of the dispute between the National Union of Mineworkers and the Government was the issue of 'economic pits' (pits are coal mines). This issue was in turn a function of how expensive it was to mine coal from British pits and how cheaply the Government could buy coal on the international market as an alternative to home supplies. Put bluntly, the price of imported coal from regions such as Eastern Europe was cheaper than that produced in British mines. There is not the space here to go into the reasons as to why this was the case (they related mainly to degree of subsidy for coal in different countries and labour costs) but British coal reserves became 'uneconomic' and ceased therefore to be usable reserves in the eyes of the Government. This translated into pits being closed down, but not without enormous resistance from the mineworkers themselves.

The UK coal miners' strike of the 1980s illustrates vividly how fundamentally political are issues of sustainability, even in relation to what one might think is a relatively straightforward question: can exploitation of a particular physical resource be maintained over time? This is why I put the word 'official' above in brackets, because many claim that the real 'heart' of the British coal dispute of the mid-1980s was the attempt by a right wing government to smash organized labour in the country, and the National Union of Mineworkers at the time symbolized the power of organized labour. This also relates to the dependency issue because the British Government wanted to reduce what it saw as over-dependence on coal as a national energy source and bring to greater prominence other sources, such as gas and nuclear fuel (which along with oil, and more recently renewable sources such as wind power, are all substitutes for coal in the UK energy mix).

Returning to copper, we can see that the issue of physical resource continuity over time is not that straightforward. But what of possible independence from the resource – in other words '*robustness*'?

It is true that there are now many substitutes for copper. Once upon a time the metal was ubiquitous in cooking utensils because of its ability to conduct heat. Over the course of the last century, these uses have tended to be substituted by other materials, such as aluminium. It would now also be very rare to find copper forming the 'dome' roof of a public building; something else would be used instead. Also, generally speaking, less of the metal is now required in the uses where it is still predominant – in other words the metal is used efficiently. To take a simple example, copper wires for conducting electricity are much 'thinner' (i.e. they contain less copper) than used to be the case. Finally, much of the copper already in use is now recycled, again making users less dependent on the primary sources (but see Box 3.4).

Box 3.4 Recycling and life cycle analysis

Any product that we use goes through a series of transformation stages from the initial extraction of the raw material through to final use of the product. These stages in the production process are shown in Figure 3.6.

The shaded boxes on the diagram indicate the various options after use. Throwing the used item away is one option, ultimately adding to the quantity of waste to be disposed of by incineration or to landfill. Re-use of the product is a possibility in some instances – glass bottles are the classic example – where the product is simply re-used in its existing form; no reprocessing is involved. Alternatively, the used product could be recycled by returning it to an earlier stage for re-incorporation into the production process.

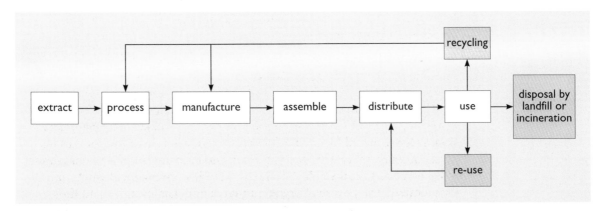

Figure 3.6 Stages in the production process of a manufactured product.

Figure 3.7 The waste hierarchy.

These options for waste management can be placed in a hierarchy, depending on their environmental impacts as shown in Figure 3.7. Better than any of the above is to avoid the problem by not producing any waste, or at least minimizing it, so waste reduction comes at the top of the hierarchy.

The hierarchy can be expanded into a sequence of options (Porteous, 2000):

1 Do not create the waste product in the first place.

2 If there is a waste product, re-use it.

3 If it cannot be re-used, then recover, reclaim or recycle the primary material in some way, if there is an environmental benefit.

4 If this is not practicable, then recover it for secondary materials or, if combustible, use it for fuel.

5 If none of these is practicable, the waste has to be disposed of by whichever disposal option has the least environmental impact.

Note the qualifying phrase for option 3, the recycle option, which is '*if there is an environmental benefit*'. Recycling is not always the answer to reducing environmental impact. The costs, both environmental and economic, of the recycling process must be taken into account. If long-distance transportation of materials is required, or if the reprocessing itself has a high energy demand or is potentially polluting, then the overall impact of recycling may be greater than disposal.

Assessing the relative merits of recycling against other disposal routes is part of life cycle analysis (LCA). LCA is a method for evaluating the whole life of a product in terms of its environmental impact. It is also known as cradle to grave analysis. LCA includes all the stages outlined in Figure 3.7, starting with the impacts arising from extracting and processing raw materials, followed by impacts from manufacturing and delivering a product. This is followed by the impacts involved in using the product and, finally, what happens at the end of the product's life – whether it is re-used, recycled or disposed of. The main purpose of LCA is to identify where improvements can be made to reduce the environmental impact of a product: for example, by comparing the relative impacts of recycling and disposal.

The technical options involving substitution, efficiency of resource use and recycling shown in Box 3.4 can in theory be measured over time to give an idea of the sustainability of copper as a resource, and in particular an idea of how sustainable is the human activity that makes use of copper.

The third of our criteria concerns *effectiveness*. One can argue that exploiting ever-lower grades of ores at greater environmental costs (see Box 3.1) does not constitute effective sustenance of copper as a resource. That aspect of effectiveness is relatively easy to measure, but there are other, much more subjective, aspects. What, for example, of those whose livelihoods depend on being paid for their labour in mining the resource? Such livelihoods might be sustained by beating down wages in order to keep labour costs low and thus reduce the cost of copper production so that it can be sold more competitively. This may contribute to *efficient* extraction of copper in monetary terms (see Box 3.2) but does it constitute *effective* sustainability of livelihoods? That very much depends on one's standpoint. Some may argue that keeping down labour costs ensures employment and does therefore effectively sustain livelihoods. Others, however, will argue that the quality of those livelihoods is deteriorating and copper miners generally are in poverty. As mentioned above, once one dimension of sustainability (e.g. environmental sustainability) becomes enmeshed with another dimension (e.g. livelihood sustainability), measuring effectiveness becomes pretty sticky. Agreeing what is effective and what is not effective is no easy task.

Table 3.1 attempts to summarize the above discussion of assessing sustainability related to copper. It draws out three contexts: the sustainability of copper as a physical resource; the sustainability of the uses to which copper is put; and the sustainability of livelihoods relating to extracting copper. It examines these in terms of our criteria – continuity over time and robustness, and effectiveness – but note that it does not treat these as discrete criteria, but rather as an overlapping spectrum.

Table 3.1 Assessing the sustainability of copper

Criteria for Sustainability	Contexts for sustainability		
	The physical resource	Uses of the resource	Livelihoods associated with extracting the resource
Continuity over time	Is it running out, and over what timescale?	How expensive is copper and what are the likely trends?	Is there/will there be a continuing need for labour?
Robustness		Can it be substituted? Can it be used more efficiently? Can it be recycled?	Are there/will there be alternative jobs available?
Effectiveness	How effectively can it be extracted? (Here effectiveness may well be conflated with efficiency – the most amount of pure copper per unit input of ore)		What wages can workers expect to receive now and in the future?

Activity 7

There are two major difficulties in attempting to measure the elements in Table 3.1. Reflect on what these might be before reading on.

Comment

One problem is that of time. Sustainability is not a static state but has to be measured over a period. Things change over time. The technologies for extracting copper, the availability of substitute materials, the means of securing livelihoods, and so on, all change. This makes assessing sustainability at a given point notoriously difficult as it involves predicting the future and, generally, we don't have enough information with which to predict the future. Often we try and extrapolate historical trends to give us a prediction, but if this is done crudely, terrible mistakes can be made.

For example, in the 1970s the influential 'Club of Rome' (see Box 1.1) predicted that by the beginning of the twenty-first century many of the physical resources on which we depend will have run out. This hasn't happened. The problem with their prediction was that its baseline assumed a crude 'business-as-usual' scenario, extrapolating past trends in the exploitation of physical resources (which showed exponential increases in exploitation) into the future. A more sophisticated prediction might take into account changing technologies in the extraction of the resource and changes in the demand for it brought about by supply and demand factors, substitute availability, efficiency of use and recycling (where appropriate). We might then get a rather different prediction which shows demand falling over time and extraction of the resource following suit.

Forecasts of the future now normally consist of a range of scenarios containing different assumptions about what the influences are likely to be. Most of the assumptions that we have hinted at above are technological and economic (e.g. extraction technologies will change; substitutes for copper will become even more widespread; demand for the resource will change), but they could be social: for example, people might come to believe that it is unacceptable to exploit our physical resources so readily.

The second problem in attempting to measure the elements in Table 3.1 is that they are inter-related with direct and indirect influences on each other. Separating them out, therefore, can be a daunting task. For example, it is not hard to see that the continuing availability of copper influences and is influenced in turn by the technological innovations that create substitutes for its uses.

How can we disentangle these inter-relationships? What we need is a tool for finding our way around the different elements and showing how they link up. We usually call such a tool for finding our way around a 'map'. Maps of course come in many shapes and forms and we are all most familiar with those that help us find our way around a 'space' – be it a city, a country, or a mountain. In *Study Guide 1*, however, you will have used concept maps to help you find your way around the key ideas in the chapters of the Course Book.

In *Study Guide 1* concept maps are referred to as conceptual frameworks.

Activity 8
Quickly cover up Figure 3.8 below. Then attempt your own concept map for exploring the sustainability issues associated with copper. Hint: take as your starting point the three contexts that formed the basis of Table 3.1 Compare your own map with that in Figure 3.8(a).

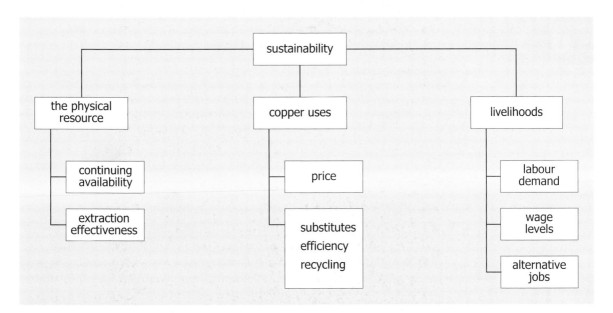

Figure 3.8 (a) Exploring the sustainability issues associated with copper. (a) The concept map. (Note the use of the term 'efficiency' under copper uses. Copper here is an input to, say, a wire carrying electricity or some other appliance. Efficiency means that the goal is to incorporate the least amount of copper for the particular use to which the metal is put.)

Sustainability of copper

1   The physical resource

1.1 Continuing availability

1.2 Extraction effectiveness

2   Copper uses

2.1 Price

2.2 Substitutes, efficiency and recycling

3   Livelihoods

3.1 Labour demand

3.2 Wage levels

3.3 Alternative jobs

Figure 3.8 (b) The concept map turned into a structure for an essay or report.

Concept maps, such as the one shown in Figure 3.8(a), are useful when trying to analyse the main ideas that might make up a 'super-concept' like sustainability. Thus, I am essentially saying that when examining sustainability issues associated with a physical resource such as copper I would do so in terms of the elements in Figure 3.8(a). If I were writing an essay or report on the subject the map could easily be turned into a set of headings and subheadings which would provide the basic structure of my work (whether I literally used them as headings and subheadings in the finished product or not), as shown in Figure 3.8(b).

Maps are chosen to depict certain essential features that you need to find your way around. So it is important to know what the concept map will *not* do: it is not good at showing many of the cross-linkages as it would become hopelessly complicated, and it does not show directly what influences what. One way to do the latter is to take an element from the concept map and try to map the various influences on that element. A tool for doing this is called a multiple cause diagram, the basic feature of which is to use arrowheads to indicate the influences (Box 3.5 gives a fuller explanation of how to construct multiple cause diagrams).

Figure 3.9 is a multiple cause diagram of the influences on development of substitutes, and more efficient use and recycling of copper. Note that:

■ the arrows do not necessarily mean (despite the title 'multiple cause') that one element causes something to happen, but more that they influence its happening. The influences can work both positively and negatively. Thus, in Figure 3.9, a rising cost of copper may contribute positively towards development of substitutes, etc., whereas a falling cost may have a negative influence on such development;

■ many of the arrows go both ways between elements indicating two-way rather than one-way influences.

Box 3.5 Constructing multiple cause diagrams

A multiple cause diagram is used to explore why something happens (such as the development of substitutes, and more efficient use and recycling of copper). The basic elements are:

- The 'something' that you are exploring.
- The influences on that 'something'.
- Lines with arrowheads that show the direction of the influence.

Note that the influences may be direct influences or they may work through another influence. For example, if you are exploring the causes of lung cancer, smoking is a direct cause, but 'lifestyle' may be a cause of smoking. This particular chain of causal events, therefore, may be represented as:

lifestyle → smoking → lung cancer

Also, the influences may work both ways (i.e. they reinforce each other) – as shown by some of the arrows going both ways in Figure 3.9.

When constructing a multiple cause diagram it is usual to start with the 'something' that you are exploring and work backwards.

Also, your multiple cause diagram should always have a defining title, as in Figure 3.9.

(Adapted from Open University course T552 *Systems Thinking and Practice*).

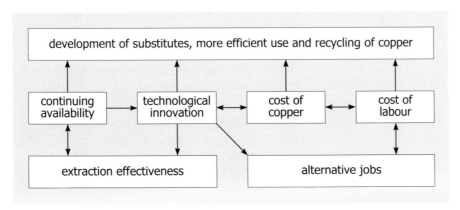

Figure 3.9 Multiple cause diagram of the influences on developing substitutes, and more efficient use and recycling of copper.

I have not drawn in all the possible arrows, only those that I consider to be most important for finding my way around. As with all maps, there is therefore a strong subjective element and your own map may well be different. In the end, maps are very personal entities – whatever way helps you to find your way around.

Activity 9

Examine Figure 3.9 and ensure that you understand it. Also note areas (if any) where you disagree with the depiction, giving reasons for your disagreement. Now rearrange the elements in Figure 3.8 to show the influences on the continuing availability of copper. When you have done this compare your answer with mine in Figure 3.10. Again note any differences and try to explain them.

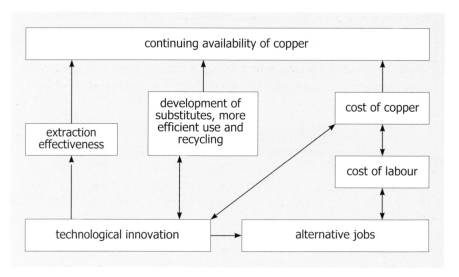

Figure 3.10 Multiple cause diagram of influences on the continuing availability of copper.

One danger with multiple cause diagrams is their tendency to relate all the elements to one (e.g. continuing availability of copper), which then inevitably is the focus of the investigation. This can mitigate against the holistic approach that is often needed when examining sustainability issues. With this caveat, however, multiple cause diagrams can be a useful means of navigating your way around the various elements of sustainability.

Note the role of technological innovation in both Figures 3.9 and 3.10. It is the mechanism through which more effective extraction, substitutes, more efficient use of the resource, recycling and alternative jobs are created. The key presence of technological innovation testifies to the crucial importance of human creativity in the sustainability debate and the consequent, perennial difficulty of stating with certainty what the future will look like (Box 3.6).

Applying the criteria: (b) the sustainability of social development action

Activity 10

Imagine that a low-income country is receiving international aid over five years in order to support its health system. What would you examine in order to assess the sustainability issues associated with the international aid?

Box 3.6 Technological innovation

Technological innovation is about bringing new products and processes into use, typically for the market. The words 'into use' are important, because it is the use to which new ideas (or inventions) are put that gives them value and turns them into innovations.

An important feature of technological innovation is *learning*. Learning can take place from formal research and development (R&D) activity, but more often it results from observation and experience – of what has gone before and of what has happened elsewhere. Learning from observation and experience translates into innovation when it results in successful 'new', or adaptations of old, products and processes being introduced. Learning will be explored again in relation to sustainability later in this text.

Comment

In terms of continuity over time I would want to check that the improvements taking place as a result of the international aid could continue after the aid stops. Thus, I would look to see how much of the aid was subsidizing drug and capital equipment expenditure or wages of health sector employees and what mechanisms were in place for replacing this money once it was no more. I would also examine how much of the aid was being spent on what might loosely be termed capacity building – strengthening management systems within the health service and improving the skills of personnel.

With respect to robustness I would check how dependent the health service was on expatriates to provide skilled labour, and again to what extent these expatriates were transferring their skills to the local personnel. I would also check whether the health service was obtaining its financial resources from a variety of sources and that the international aid was not an especially high percentage of the overall budget.

Finally, with respect to effectiveness, I would want to check out the quality of the health service and what was being sustained. This would overlap with other criteria. For example, one plan might be to sustain any improvements brought about by international aid via cost recovery.* If that aid was withdrawn, it might mean that poor people would be excluded from those improvements because they could not afford to pay for them. If the aid were dominating the country's health budget and was tending to influence policy away from what had been internally decided towards a policy that suited donor priorities (e.g. away from a primary health care policy towards more curative-based policies – see Chapter 4 of the Course Book), I would similarly be concerned. Overall, I would want to check that the aid was helping to reinforce the entire health system of the country, rather than just that aspect on which the international aid might be targeted.

*In this context, cost recovery means charging health system users for the treatment they receive, e.g. charges for medical prescriptions. (Note the cost recovery charges will seldom cover the whole cost of the treatment.)

I have quoted previously from LaFond (1995). At the end of her article, which is titled 'Sustaining primary health care', she notes three possible contradictions with respect to international aid, all of which resonate with the comment on Activity 10 above (LaFond, 1995, pp.35–37):

1   Immediate needs or capacity building: here LaFond cites the example of using international aid to provide universal child

immunization in a poor country, rather than using that aid to improve the overall capacity of the health system. Clearly the latter helps build a sustainable health system, whereas the former serves an immediate and pressing need and one doesn't worry about what will happen to immunization levels once the funding is withdrawn.

2   Dependency or robustness: LaFond notes that in Nepal (a very poor country) the annual health expenditure is approximately US$1 per head of population. This is a very small sum and LaFond notes that the 'government cannot afford to sustain the current health infrastructure nor support greater service expansion. It therefore depends on external support'. She goes on to say that Nepal simply does not have a sufficient resource base to sustain an adequate health service by itself and it must therefore 'accept its financial dependency on donors'. But does this mean that it also has to accept loss of control over priority setting in health, which are overly influenced by donor agendas?

3   Conflicting goals of effectiveness versus continuity and robustness. Again, LaFond cites the example of immunization campaigns financed by donors, where 'tight' delivery by streamlined teams and special staff can be very efficient in the short term, but do little for longer term sustainability which might involve institutionalizing immunization within existing structures. Donors, however, will want to see a rapid 'return' on their money in, for example, increased immunization coverage and declining child mortality over a short period of time (say 3–5 years). They are less concerned about whether these improvements will last into the future.

Balancing the criteria: the Index of Sustainable and Economic Welfare

We have examined the criteria for assessing sustainability in terms of a physical resource (copper) and social development (health). Even if we can measure continuity, robustness and effectiveness (and the discussion above shows that such measurement is by no means straightforward), how do we balance them in order to make a definitive statement about sustainability? What should take precedence – continuity and robustness, or effectiveness? This is the third of the contradictions that LaFond points out above. Also, how might we balance the different dimensions and contexts of sustainability, such as environmental, social and economic sustainability? In other words, how might we judge sustainability more holistically?

One way of doing this is to develop a composite index (Box 3.7) where assumptions about the various balances that need to be struck are combined into a common 'currency' which then provides a single figure (the index) of sustainability. The common 'currency' is often economic – all the elements of sustainability to be considered and balanced are given an economic value in US$ or £sterling or another international currency.

Box 3.7 Indices

Indices are the plural of index! An index is a way of putting something into order, as in the index to the Course Book or a library catalogue, which are both done by alphabetical sequence. Similarly, a numerical index is a way of ordering numbers according to some 'rule' which enables you to observe patterns that may be of interest to you.

To construct a numerical index it is usual first to define a baseline number against which all others are compared. This is best illustrated by an example. Below I construct a 'child mortality' index, based on Table 4.2 of Chapter 4 in the Course Book. This table shows under-five (child) mortality rates for selected countries for the years 1960 and 1997.

Step 1. Define the purpose of the index: in this case I want it to show relative trends in child mortality of different countries between 1960 and 1997.

Step 2. Define your baseline. In this case it will be the under-five mortality rate in 1960.

Step 3. Give your baseline a number which forms the baseline index. It's usually sensible to choose a commonly known number. In this case, I am defining the index for child mortality for all countries in 1960 as 1.0. This is the same as dividing the actual under-five mortality rate for a country by itself for the year 1960. Thus, for example, Tanzania had an under-five mortality rate in 1960 of 240 deaths per 1000 live births. 240/240 = 1.0, which is the child mortality index for 1960. China had a child mortality rate of 209 per thousand live births in 1960, and its index also equals 1.0 (209/209) because we are defining the index for all countries as being the same at 1960.

Step 4. Calculate the index for subsequent years (in this case the only subsequent year is 1997). Following our previous example, Tanzania's under-five mortality rate in 1997 was 143. The child mortality index for this year is then obtained by dividing this figure by the 1960 under-five mortality rate for Tanzania: 143/240 = 0.6. China's under-five mortality rate in 1997 was 47, and its index is similarly obtained: 47/209 = 0.2.

What does all this tell us? Nothing about actual under-five mortality rates because we have massaged the figures! But the indices do reveal useful things. Let us tabulate our calculations as follows:

	Child mortality index	
	1960	*1997*
Tanzania	1.0	0.6
China	1.0	0.2

This table tells us that child mortality indices of both countries have fallen between 1960 and 1997, revealing improvements in child mortality over that period. However, China's child mortality has fallen three times more than that of Tanzania (0.6/0.2 = 3). We could repeat the exercise for all 26 countries in Table 4.2 of the Course Book and it would provide us with an easy comparison of how different countries have improved with respect to child mortality since 1960. It does not show us where countries 'are at', but how far they 'have come' since 1960 from different starting positions.

You have used another index already in U213 – the Human Development Index in the *Introduction to Poverty and Inequality*. This also uses 1.0 as a baseline, but here it is not connected to time. Rather, it is used to compare countries at a given moment. 1.0 is the highest Human Development Index that may be achieved by a country, and all other countries have indices that are in relation to this 'best' figure (i.e. they are all below 1.0, and may be ranked on this basis).

The Human Development Index is also an example of a *composite* index – one that combines different factors (in this case utility derived from income, life expectancy and educational attainment). This is a particularly good use of an index, because it's a way of combining factors that may have different 'currencies' (e.g. income is measured by US dollars and life expectancy by years).

The Human Development Index was devised by the United Nations Development Programme (UNDP) in 1990 as an alternative measure of development to that based on income alone (where we might use gross national product, GNP, per capita). The Index of Economic and Sustainable Welfare (ISEW) used in this text is, like the Human Development Index, a composite index that has been developed as an alternative to the purely economic measure of gross domestic product (GDP) per capita. One point about the ISEW, however, is that it does not operate from a common baseline index. Instead, it is calculated in a monetary currency, such as US dollars or pounds sterling, so that it may be compared directly with GDP per capita as Figures 3.11 and 3.12 in the text below show.

It is best to illustrate a 'sustainability index' by reference to a specific example again, this time from the UK. The draft National Park Management Plan (NPMP) for the Pembrokeshire Coast in the UK claims that quality of life in the UK has conventionally been defined in purely economic terms, specifically economic output or gross domestic product (GDP*) averaged across the population (GDP per capita). An increasing GDP has generally been seen as sustaining and improving quality of life.

*GDP is defined in Chapter 1 of the Course Book.

The draft NPMP takes issue with this, however, suggesting that quality of life has to be viewed more holistically:

Defining well-being through Gross Domestic Product has led to 'sustainable development' being interpreted as 'business as usual'. We need to develop more comprehensive measures of our long term economic, social and environmental well-being.

(NPMP, 2000, p.4)

Drawing on the work of the New Economics Foundation in the UK, the NPMP introduces the Index of Sustainable Economic Welfare (ISEW), which it says offers a 'better picture of the costs and benefits of the economy ... ISEW recognizes for example the costs of pollution on health; takes account of resource depletion; counts the cost of car accidents. On the benefit side, ISEW acknowledges the value of unpaid work, for example' (NPMP, 2000, p.4).

In terms of our previous criteria, therefore, the ISEW attempts to establish a measure for *effective* well-being over *time* (Figure 3.11).

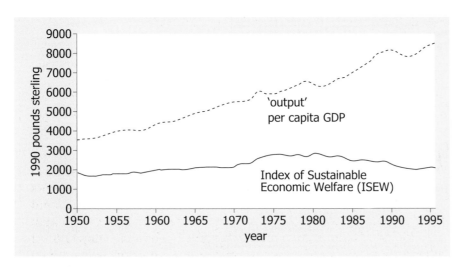

Figure 3.11 GDP and ISEW in the UK: 1950–1996.

Activity 11

Examine Figure 3.11 and compare the ISEW and GDP per capita for the UK over time.

1 What has been the broad trend of GDP per capita over the period 1950–1996?

2 What has been the broad trend of ISEW per capita over the period 1950–1996?

3 Comment briefly on the 'gap' between GDP per capita and ISEW per capita over the period 1990–1996.

Comment

Although there have been some fluctuations, GDP per capita in the UK broadly increased between 1950 and 1996. ISEW per capita also increased initially, but reached a plateau over the period mid-1970s to early 1980s, after which it has declined. ISEW has always been lower than GDP over the period (this is a function of the weighting given to economic costs referred to above in the calculation of ISEW), but more importantly, the

Line graphs such as those in Figures 3.11 and 3.12 are useful for giving you an immediate visual image of what is happening over time. If the same data had been presented to you via a table of numbers you would have had to do some work before spotting the trends outlined here, especially that of the widening gap between GDP and ISEW.

41

extent of the gap has widened significantly since around 1975. This widening gap suggests that simply increasing output does not necessarily lead to a higher quality of life; in fact it can be at the expense of quality of life.

This widening gap between GDP and ISEW is not restricted to the UK: it is a feature of many high income countries. Figure 3.12 shows a similar pattern for the US (note that this figure uses GNP rather than GDP, but the point remains the same).

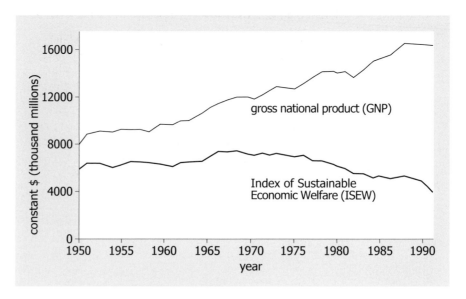

Figure 3.12 GNP and ISEW in the US: 1950–1991.

As hinted at above, composite indices such as the ISEW are compiled after certain assumptions have been made about:

■ what factors to include (some of the factors included in the ISEW are given above);

■ what relative importance or 'weight' to give to the different factors (e.g. in the ISEW, should less or greater importance be given to resource depletion than the effect of pollution on health?);

■ what economic value to assign to factors that inevitably contain an array of qualitative features (such as car accidents).

The danger is not the assumptions *per se* (they may be perfectly reasonable) but the fact that they are hidden and are not therefore subject to obvious scrutiny. What we generally see is the index – a single figure – that most people do not have the time to examine. This is an important point: numerical data do not represent 'objective facts'.

Summary of Section 3

1 Continuity over time, robustness and effectiveness can form general criteria for assessing sustainability, which can be applied to any context.

2 Continuity over time and robustness are closely related and concern the ability to extend the present into the future while having access to the necessary resources that are required for this to happen. Effectiveness is related to how successful something is in meeting stated goals. It is of little value to sustain something that is not effectively meeting its goals, but effectiveness can be notoriously difficult to capture as it can mean different things to different people.

3 Mapping techniques can be a useful method of finding one's way around the complexity of sustainability. Concept maps and multiple cause diagrams are used here. It should be noted that maps tend to record only those essential features to help you achieve what you want to do. No map represents the 'whole picture'.

4 Indices can be devised to capture sustainability in a more holistic sense. The Index of Sustainable Economic Welfare (ISEW) is introduced here to show that quality of life is much more than increasing economic output. Indices are based on hidden assumptions about the factors that are taken into account in compiling them. They are ultimately only as good as the validity of these assumptions.

4 The question of 'how'

Chapter 16 of the Course Book suggests that a 'post-Washington consensus' is emerging in relation to a 'sustainable globalization' that is 'conducive to social justice, human security and environmental protection' (p.363). Certainly, sustainability is now commonly linked to international development targets such as poverty, as the quotations you have read from the UK Department for International Development (DFID) earlier in the text indicate. Thus, there is a measure of agreement internationally over *what* is to be sustained. Less is known or agreed, however, about *how* we might do it. We examine below some possible broad mechanisms: accountability, replication and management.

4.1 Holding people and agencies responsible for their actions

Chapter 9 on development agencies in the Course Book argues that philanthropy on the part of these agencies to reduce poverty cannot be enough and concludes (p.216): 'Overall poverty reduction requires the institutionalization of altruism and for services to be provided as a right rather than from goodwill.'

By the 'institutionalization of altruism', the author means the rights of individuals and groups to hold development agencies *to account* in order for poverty reduction itself to be sustainable. In the context here, it is especially about the less powerful being able to hold to account the more powerful in the interests of development that is inclusive of everybody. Having the right to elect the government of your country (or any other group of which you are a member) is one form of accountability that may be exercised. Another form of holding the powerful to account might be through the media (although the media themselves represent other powerful interests). A third might be the formation of pressure groups on, say, the environment or education or health, which directly engage with governments and other agencies on these issues.

This issue of accountability is taken up later in the Course Book, especially in Chapter 16 'Sustainable globalization: the global politics of development and exclusion in the new world order' and Chapter 20 'Life in the cities'.

As indicated above, Chapter 16 clearly sees sustainable development in terms of justice for all people in the world. It acknowledges that achieving this is a major challenge, not least because global politics is 'still beset by significant disparities in power, influence and access to resources. In this respect the rich and powerful, whether in the North or the South, have much greater potential to set global agendas and influence the terms of globalization than do the poor and the excluded' (p.358). One can also add that there are few institutionalized mechanisms for holding rich and powerful organizations such as transnational corporations to account for their activities.

It is a challenge nevertheless that Chapter 16 believes can be, and is beginning to be, met through the management of globalization processes by both governments and citizens. Thus, the final point of the chapter summary (p.364) states: 'A crucial question for the twenty-first century is whether globalization can be managed in the interests of equity and sustainability.'

Activity 12

By what mechanisms does Chapter 16 suggest that globalization can be managed in the interests of equity and sustainability?

Comment

The chapter suggests that these fall under three headings: regulating globalization, regionalizing globalization and resisting globalization (pp.360–362). Regulating globalization concerns the use of international treaties and the establishment of international institutions. Regionalizing globalization refers to the formation of regional blocs (e.g. the European Union) that act as geopolitical entities with more influence than individual nation states. Resisting globalization examines the power and influence of 'transnational civil society' and 'globalization from below' as 'an alternative vision of development which starts from the assumption that 'all economics is local' and which seeks above all the empowerment of peoples, human security and environmental sustainability' (p.362). A few pages earlier, the chapter heralds this argument about transnational civil society by claiming that there has emerged an 'infrastructure of global politics' which has created a 'political space in which 'globalization from below' can seek to contest global agendas and bring *to account* [my emphasis] the citadels of power' (p.358).

Chapter 20 relates the issue of civil society and accountability at city level to one of the two main conditions that need to be fulfilled for cities to be sustained 'places of possibility' rather than 'enduring poverty and grind for the millions of resourceful people who grow up in them and flock to them' (p.442). One of these conditions concerns cities having 'enough political and financial autonomy to respond to the needs and demands of their citizens without financial responsibility devolving exclusively to the local level' (p.441). The other is about ensuring that 'civil society is allowed to flourish because ... it is that part of social life that is essential if responsive urban planning, inclusive urban politics and a democratic city are to exist' (p.441).

Thus a major concern of Chapters 9, 16 and 20 of the Course Book is about how those without power can hold to account those with power through a vibrant civil society. Accountability in this sense is seen as the means by which development is made to be effective in meeting needs of equity, justice, the poor, citizens and so on. It thus links to the effectiveness aspect of sustainability.

Accountability to the less powerful is also implicit in more specific and deliberate development actions, such as those that stress participation of all stakeholders, including the supposed beneficiaries of the actions. Participatory technology development (PTD), mentioned in connection with Chapter 19 of the Course Book, is a case in point. We return to issues of accountability in deliberate development action below.

4.2 Replication as learning

Chapter 14 of the Course Book charts the rise and fall of the USSR socialist model of development, arguing that it eventually became unsustainable. The argument is made mainly in terms of the effectiveness of the model over time: it was effective in mobilizing resources for the initial stages of 'extensive' industrialization, but far less effective in terms of later 'intensive' industrialization (p.317); and it was not effective in meeting the needs of the rural population (p.313) nor those who became urbanized and educated (p.317).

Another point that the chapter makes in relation to the sustainability of the Soviet model, however, is that it did not *replicate* well to other countries, particularly to China, where it largely failed to ensure industrialization and development (p.317). And, although the USSR model that gained ascendancy was based on the idea of 'socialism in one country', it nevertheless appeared to offer lessons for other countries attempting to develop and industrialize. To this extent, therefore, replication was an aim.

Replication in relation to development, whether for industrialization strategies or specific projects, is not explicitly raised elsewhere in the Course Book, although it tends to be assumed in some chapters. Thus the idea of having an active civil society as a pre-condition for both sustainable globalization and sustainable cities assumes that the condition is replicated across the world. Similarly, to the extent that a Gender and Development (GAD) approach represents an advance on a Women in Development (WID) approach in relation to gender and development action (Chapter 18), it is hoped and expected that the former might be replicated across development interventions.

Taken literally, replication by itself does not equate necessarily with sustainability, however. For example, for over 50 years in the last century the World Bank sought to replicate large infrastructure projects (such as big dams) across the world, projects which it now sees as having sustainability problems. In fact, the *failure* of replication in many cases – whether this be the failure of the Soviet model of industrialization to replicate successfully to other parts of the world, or the failure to replicate World Bank infrastructure projects successfully – has turned it into a 'dirty word' in development circles.

A more sophisticated view of replication and sustainablity has now developed, which is less to do with creating 'blueprints' from development action that can be repeated exactly elsewhere, and is more about being able to institutionalize *learning* from what is done in order to provide lessons for elsewhere. Rarely, these lessons might be that a particular development action does provide a blueprint for other places and circumstances and can be replicated exactly as a model. More often, the model is adapted to different contexts, but is based on the principles of the original. It is to the general issue of learning for sustainability that we now turn.

4.3 Management and learning

Management is about conscious processes of steering, adaptation and regulation over time in relation to defined goals. There are strong resonances, therefore, between management and the discussion above about sustainability mechanisms of holding to account and adaptive replication. Indeed, Chapter 16 of the Course Book argues explicitly that globalization has to be 'managed' if it is to meet twin concerns of equity and sustainability.

The idea that development action might provide lessons rather than exact blueprints for replication leads to a view of sustainability as a managed *action-learning* process. In this view development action is sustained by deliberate adaptation and change over time in response to learning from doing or application (a point also made in Chapter 19 of the Course Book on technology and development). Such learning is achieved through formal *monitoring and evaluation* of development interventions. Monitoring concerns routine collection of data in relation to an intervention's performance and allows for ongoing adjustment and refinement. Evaluation is seen more as an intermittent retrospective assessment (which will make use of monitoring data but also data specially collected for the evaluation) of performance in relation to the intervention's objectives.

Managed action-learning is also linked to accountability because 'to whom you are accountable' influences what you agree to assess in monitoring and evaluation exercises, how you interpret the data that results, and how you thus learn from and steer the action. It is, however, necessary to separate the reality from the rhetoric. In most aid-driven interventions for development, accountability is a key word, but it usually means accountability by those carrying out the intervention to those giving the money. This is called upwards accountability by Edwards and Hulme (1995, p.9) to the more powerful, as opposed to downwards accountability, which is accountability to the supposed beneficiaries of development interventions. Accountability issues therefore represent the point where sustainability becomes highly politicized. Arguments over what is to be sustained, how it is to be sustained, and for whose benefit are largely resolved by who has the power to hold whom to account. This is where, going beyond specific interventions, the existence of a vibrant civil society enters – as a counterweight to those with formal power, whether they are governments (local or national), large corporations or international donors and other organizations.

Replication, management and accountability are inextricably linked in development interventions, therefore, and are also linked to learning for sustainability. Learning takes place from *doing* the development intervention, but the lessons that are learned are filtered by who holds whom to account. The learning results in new interventions, or 'replication' where the latter can take various forms:

- exact replication in a new context (this is rare);
- adapted replication in a new context;
- adapted replication within the old context.

This then feeds back into 'doing' and the learning process starts again. The whole process constitutes what might be called sustainable management of the development intervention (Figure 4.1).

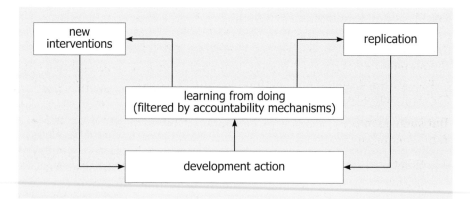

Figure 4.1 Sustainable management of development interventions.

Summary of Section 4
1 Accountability is essential if there is to be effective and sustainable development action that meets the needs of equity and social justice. Who is accountable to whom, however, is a highly political matter.
2 A broad way of ensuring accountability is to have a vibrant civil society.
3 Replication of development action is a sustainability issue: usually development interventions at any level have replication at least as an implicit aim.
4 Accountability and replication are aspects of conscious management of development action where they enable a learning process for sustainability to occur.

5 Sustainability and sustainable development

The previous three sections have examined respectively:

- multiple contexts in which the term sustainability is used;
- general criteria for assessing sustainability;
- broad mechanisms for achieving sustainability.

Although development has formed the backdrop to these sections, sustainability as a general concept rather than sustainable development as an explicit idea has been the main focus. This section switches the focus somewhat to explore that explicit idea. In so doing it introduces a framework that combines four different contexts of sustainability which can be used to develop an integrative and holistic approach towards sustainable development. It also indicates the relevance to the framework of the general criteria and broad mechanisms for achieving sustainability that we have explored.

The first section in this text suggested that sustainable development is simply the application of the broad concept of sustainability to development. Thus, in terms of the basic criteria for assessing sustainability that we developed earlier, we might define sustainable development as the effective development of a society or country that is continued over time while maintaining access to the inputs of resources that it requires.

But such a simple formulation of sustainable development begs two fundamental questions:

1   What do we mean by *effective* development? I shall return to this below.

2   A more general question relates to the meaning of *development*. Thus, to draw the Course Book distinction (Chapter 2), are we referring to the sustainability of development processes, or the sustainability of deliberate actions aimed at development? Both uses are, of course, valid, but the literature tends to refer only to the former as sustainable development, with the latter being more specifically part of the means by which it might be achieved.

In this second regard, therefore, sustainable globalization (Chapter 16) and sustainable cities (Chapter 20) are aspects of sustainable development as they relate to broad processes (globalization) or entities (cities). Similarly, the idea of a vibrant civil society calling the powerful to account, so that 'needs' such as equity and ecological sustainability are met, is associated with sustainable development. An intervention, however, to improve the livelihoods of, for example, poor women in a specific location, which solicits the participation of the women in conceptualizing, designing and implementing the intervention, is more directly to do with the sustainability of that particular action.

The idea that deliberate actions aimed at development are 'means' that contribute towards the 'end' of sustainable development is pervasive. We have to be careful about applying it too rigorously, however, because one can always ask the question: 'Where do ends end?' If, as the previous section suggested, we take a learning process view of sustainable development, as well of sustainability, there is no end – or rather each 'end' becomes a means to something that is perhaps even broader. This is perhaps best illustrated by a hypothetical example.

Imagine a poor area of a city in a developing country, where infectious diseases are rife and where the inhabitants are campaigning for the establishment of a decent sanitation infrastructure. This 'public health' action may achieve its 'end' of the eventual establishment of a sustainable sanitation infrastructure, but it may also raise other development issues for the campaigners during the course of their struggle. The success of their campaign may then give them the confidence to attempt to influence these other issues – in other words the campaign might contribute to the vibrancy of civil society in the city. This vibrant civil society in turn contributes to the city being a place of opportunity, which leads to further development actions and so on.

I argued in the last section that conscious management is required to achieve any kind of sustainability. 'Management' implies the need for clarity in the vision of what one is trying to achieve and purposeful engagement in achieving it. Let us now apply these ideas to the 'classic' definition of sustainable development, which was provided by the World Commission on Environment and Development (WCED) in 1987 and which has been briefly discussed in earlier sections. In this definition the vision comprises 'development that meets the needs of the present without compromising the ability of future generations to meet their needs' (Brundtland, 1987). Effective development then becomes that which successfully meets this vision. But whose and what needs are we talking about? This Introduction, and the Course Book, place a good deal of emphasis on social equity and ecological sustainability as broad 'needs' – but, as also mentioned earlier, a common criticism of the WCED statement is that it appears to assume social homogeneity within present and future generations. This is clearly not the case and different societal groups will claim different needs.

To be fair, in the book *Our Common Future*, in which the above definition appears, Brundtland does state that she is particularly concerned with the needs of the world's poor. And later definitions of sustainable development have explicitly taken on board the issue of social equity within both present and future generations. For example:

> To promote development that enhances the natural and built environment in ways that are compatible with:
>
> > the requirement to conserve, even increase overall the stock of natural assets;

the need to avoid damaging the regenerative capacity of the world's natural ecosystems;

the need to achieve greater social equality;

the avoidance of passing additional costs and risks to succeeding generations.

(Blowers, 1993)

Unless we operationalize the equity concern, however, through active management, sustainable development runs the risk of being for the few at the expense of the many (and hence not socially equitable nor ecologically sustainable for the many). Also, management implies a constant steering and learning process that takes cognisance of the context in which it takes place. This is the mechanism by which 'the needs of future generations' (or inter-generational equity) can be secured.

We can consider two senses in which management for sustainable development may be made active:

1   Attempts to manage broad processes directly, in the name of stated goals such as equity and ecological sustainability.

2   Deliberate actions for sustainability (and which are considered to contribute towards sustainable development) on the part of various agencies.

Let us consider these in turn.

5.1 Attempts to manage broad processes directly

This is very much the argument in Chapter 16 of the Course Book for achieving sustainable globalization in the name of identified goals of equity and ecological sustainability. Chapter 16 also considers *agency* – in other words, *who* is going to manage the globalization process? The answer to this question is covered in the Comment to Activity 12 in the previous section, where the agents identified in Chapter 16 are:

■ International organizations that might regulate the globalization process. This function might conceivably be mandated to an existing organization, such as the United Nations, or possibly a new organization might be set up by nation states.

■ Nation states who might co-operate in regional blocs.

■ An emerging transnational civil society that might apply pressure from below.

The notion of non-market intervention in Chapter 2 (pp.45–47) of the Course Book provides us with another illustration of attempts to manage the transformation processes associated with industrial capitalism. As with Chapter 16, the goals of such interventionism are social and ecological.

Now refer to Chapter 22 of the Course Book. A large part of this chapter is about genetically modified (GM) crops, where the question is asked: 'Feeding the world – or the market?' (Section 22.2). Section 22.3 then describes three 'visions' for the future of GM crops. Two of these might be described as different visions for 'managing' the market. Identify the two visions and describe the basic premises on which each operates.

Comment

The two 'management' visions are 'The regulated market vision' (pp.480–482) and 'The partnership and networking vision' (pp.482–484). (The third is the free market vision which makes no claims to manage the market in any active sense.)

The regulated market vision is essentially about international agreements to regulate GM development, using as an instrument the precautionary principle.

The partnership and networking vision is about sharing of 'information, knowledge and experience' between North and South, between public and private sectors, and between researchers and local producers. It is essentially about both 'feeding the world and the market', and the authors suggest (p.484):

'New models of research and partnering hold out the promise of access to knowledge and experience which could enable a narrowing of the gap in capabilities between richer and poorer countries. And domestically based networks could begin to develop advanced biotechnology into crops grown by local poor farmers.'

Section 22.3 outlines the possibilities for, examples of, and constraints on, each of the visions and you should familiarize yourself with these if you have not already done so.

The final chapter of the Course Book, Chapter 24, provides a neat link back to the discussion of intervention in global industrial capitalism contained in Chapter 2 and mentioned briefly above. This is the section on 'Ecologically sustainable industrialization' (pp.520–522), which is based on a book by David Wallace, from the International Energy Agency in Paris (Wallace, 1996). Wallace's main argument is as follows:

1   (Ecological) sustainability is basically about the structure of industrialization, which therefore must be actively managed and not left to 'the market'.

2   Transformation of the structure of industrialization has historically taken place in rapidly developing locations. Thus the craft structure of early British industrialization was transformed by the US in the late nineteenth and early twentieth centuries to the Fordist structure of mass production, large factories, economies of scale and an intensive division of labour. The 'just-in-time, flexible' structure was pioneered by Japan from the 1960s.

3   These transformations in the structure of industrialization are able to occur because of the development of new technologies and new institutions. In fact, one of Wallace's key points is that the Fordist structure could not have been initiated in Britain because of entrenched institutional interests in maintaining the craft structure.

For similar reasons, 'just-in-time, flexible' structures which are taking over from Fordism could not have been initiated in the US.

4   This is why, Wallace argues, the most promising locations for structures based on ecological sustainability to emerge are not in the countries that have already industrialized, but in rapidly developing countries of the South, where the institutional barriers to new structures are relatively few. This flies in the face of the conventional wisdom that the North should take the lead in this area, transferring the necessary technologies to the South.

5   It is, therefore, despite much argument to the contrary, more possible to steer industrialization in the South towards ecological sustainability. Wallace further claims, and this is where his argument becomes weaker, that foreign investment in developing countries can be a mechanism for such sustainable industrialization. Multinational corporations (MNCs) have the technologies and capacity to be able to conduct their operations in a sustainable way; what is needed is leverage via institutional structures set up by Southern governments that ensure they do so. Wallace claims that such institutions are unlikely to scare off investment by MNCs who are desperately seeking expanding markets for their goods and services in developing countries.

6   Although Wallace attempts to answer, therefore, the obvious question raised in Chapter 24 (p.521): '...why would MNCs engage in the way [Wallace] envisions?', it is not true at present that all countries in the South offer the prospect of large markets, and the leverage of poorer and less populous countries is consequently very limited. Also, as Chapter 24 (p.521) points out: '...why would developing countries adopt this agenda, when some of them feel understandably reluctant to bear the brunt of having to make drastic changes, when it is industrialized countries which have created the [ecological sustainability] problem?' (Figure 5.1).

Figure 5.1 Steel foundry at Letchworth, UK, in the 1920s.

Wallace's argument nevertheless illustrates two important points in the sustainability debate:

1 Sustainable development is something that requires conscious and constant management or intervention.

2 New technologies are needed but are not enough. Institutions – or the 'rules of the game' (Box 2.1) – that set the overall framework for management are needed too.

Industrialization is about the way society is organized to exploit physical, biological and environmental resources (Box 3.1) to provide the goods and services that it requires – hence Wallace's concerns about ecological sustainability. And, of course, it is through technologies and institutions that such exploitation occurs. This provides us with a simple framework for analysing prospects for sustainable industrialization (Figure 5.2).

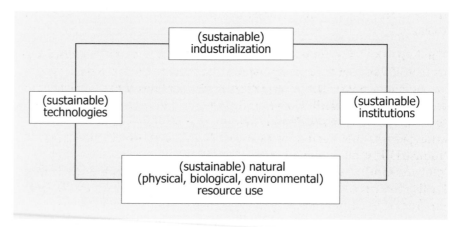

Figure 5.2 A framework for analysing prospects for sustainable industrialization.

Given that they do comprise an important feature of our framework, before leaving this subsection it is worthwhile considering a few examples of institutional arrangements that are claimed as templates for sustainable development. In *Introduction to Transitions* you will have seen that markets are essentially 'rules of the game' and, moreover, that markets are 'made' – in other words they are social institutions. Thus markets are an obvious and ubiquitous example of institutional frameworks within which we use technologies to exploit physical resources.

Activity 14

(a) The idea of 'market mechanisms forming the institutional frameworks for sustainable development' forms the basis of which view that is described in Chapter 7 of the Course Book?

(b) Which two other kinds of institutional frameworks for sustainable development are described in Chapter 7 and what are their main features?

Comment

The answer to (a) is fairly obvious – it is the neoliberal view. The chapter then describes two other views that might form the bases of institutional frameworks for sustainable development (question b):

1   The 'people-centred' view, where the institutional framework would be based on the primacy of local control over resources and local participation in decision-making. In this view, the (local) community is the social institution.

2   The global environmental management view, where the institutional framework, or rules of the game, is negotiated between the various stakeholders and then enshrined in treaties or protocols, e.g. the Montreal Protocol on ozone depletion.

Your work on the making of markets in *Introduction to Transitions* will have alerted you to the fact that markets are not socially neutral. It should be noted, however, that neither of these alternatives to the market is socially neutral either. The primacy of the local is likely to mean the primacy of local élites, just as international treaties and protocols are likely to reflect the relative bargaining powers of different country stakeholders.

The framework shown in Figure 5.2 is a 'tool' for analysis. It suggests to us that, if we wish to assess prospects for sustainable industrialization, we have to examine the exploitation of physical resources through technologies and institutional arrangements. Just as there are different technologies, so too are there different possible institutional arrangements that need to be assessed. In this framework, moreover, 'industrialization' is interchangeable with other processes, such as 'globalization' – where again we need to look at the exploitation of the Earth's natural resources through technologies and institutions. In fact, the framework can be employed at different levels to examine the contribution towards sustainable development of managing both broad transformation processes and specific, positive development interventions.

5.2 Deliberate development actions on the part of various agencies

Deliberate action for development is invariably about promoting livelihoods in one form or another, either directly (e.g. creating opportunities for economic activity), or indirectly (e.g. providing physical infrastructure such as roads or infrastructure services such as health and education). In fact some agencies – the United Nations Development Programme and the UK's Department for International Development being prime examples – try to place their activity within what they call a 'sustainable livelihoods' framework to the extent that this becomes a working definition of sustainable development.

Chapter 7 of the Course Book makes the explicit link between livelihoods and the environment, and the chapter's summary (p.162) states:

> ...to understand environmental degradation, we need to consider people's livelihoods, for these establish the relationship between economic activity and environment.

Earlier in the chapter (p.149) the statement is made that 'All human activity exploits the environment' through the use of (a) natural resources as raw materials, and (b) the environment to accept waste products. It goes on to say that 'The intensity of exploitation of these resources determines the environmental consequences, in terms of the depletion of non-renewable resources and degradation of renewable resources.'

Although the emphasis in Chapter 7 is on economic activity, the term 'livelihoods' means much more than this and in fact has strong social connotations. At its simplest, a livelihood is the means of living, but much depends on what we mean by 'living'. Broadly speaking, 'living' concerns the satisfaction of needs, which brings us back to our WCED (Brundtland) definition of sustainable development and the discussion above about needs. Very few would argue that 'living' is equivalent to satisfying only survival needs of food and shelter. Most people would add various combinations of, or adaptations to, the list of 'human-needs centred development' given on p.34 of the Course Book. This is essentially a 'social' list of needs, with its emphases on low levels of poverty, equity and education.

Activity 15

Quickly remind yourself of the human-needs centred development list on p.34 of the Course Book.

This list can also be described as providing the elements of what constitutes 'living' in a broad sense beyond mere survival. Interventions to promote livelihoods then become the means by which we secure the list. Livelihoods as a set of means form the basis of the definition adopted by several international aid agencies. For example:

> A livelihood comprises the capabilities, assets and activities required for a means of living.

(DFID, 1999a)

*The *Introduction to Poverty and Inequality* contains a further discussion of capability.

Capabilities in the above definition comprise the ability to do things with (i.e. manage) one's assets.* Personal assets in turn include: skills and knowledge, good health, and access to basic infrastructure, social, financial and physical resources. DFID and other agencies aren't only interested in interventions, however, that promote livelihoods as a snapshot at a single point in time. They are interested in how they are best sustained over time. Thus, the DFID definition just quoted adds:

> A livelihood is sustainable when it can cope with and recover from stresses and shocks and maintain or enhance its capabilities and assets both now and in the future, while not undermining the natural resource base.
>
> (DFID, 1999a)

A sustainable livelihood for DFID, therefore, also incorporates sustaining a 'natural' (physical, biological and environmental) resource base, which resonates with the argument in Chapter 7 of the Course Book and summarized above. But this statement on its own begs the question of 'How?'. 'How do (sustainable) livelihood activities exploit resources (sustainably)?'

This is where the framework for analysing the sustainable management of broad processes such as industrialization and globalization, as discussed in the last subsection, can again prove useful. In order to exploit physical, biological and environmental resources for livelihoods, we employ technologies in their most general sense – both the hardware and software (human knowledge and skills) aspects of technologies. That is almost a statement of the obvious. But the way in which we use technologies to exploit these resources is within an institutional framework, which again determines the 'rules of the game'.

In the previous subsection, we examined two of the alternative institutional arrangements to markets discussed in Chapter 7 of the Course Book – based on the 'people-centred' and 'global environmental management' of sustainable development. These views are separated by level of application in Chapter 7: the former applies to the local, the latter to international levels. But environmental management occurs at the local level too, especially when related to deliberate interventions that involve outside donors. Moreover, the institutional arrangements for local environmental management often then appear to incorporate the people-centred view within a management framework. Thus the institutional arrangements for managing DFID's sustainable livelihoods programmes are expected to include (DFID, 1999b):

- people-centredness, which DFID describes as focusing support on what matters to people, understands the differences between them and 'works with them in a way that is congruent with their current livelihood strategies, social environment and ability to adapt';

- responsive and participatory practices so that poor people themselves are 'key actors in identifying and addressing livelihood priorities'.

Figure 5.3 is a simple adaptation of Figure 5.2, to show how we might examine the contribution of deliberate development interventions to sustainable development.

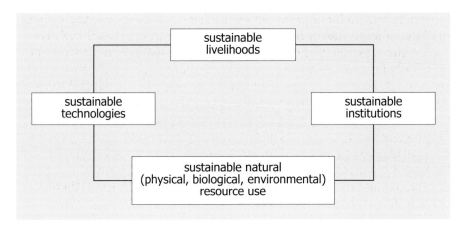

Figure 5.3 Conceptual framework for analysing the contribution of deliberate interventions towards sustainable development.

5.3 Applying the framework

Figure 5.3 is a fairly abstract framework, and the rest of this section shows how it might be applied, therefore, to a couple of real attempts at intervention to promote sustainable development. These two examples are at different levels – one international, the other 'local'.

Global climate change negotiations

You should first read Box 7.1 'Managing the global commons: atmospheric pollution' on pp.142–144 of the Course Book, which sets the context for the following account. Concentrate on those sections of Box 7.1 that deal with the greenhouse effect.

The global climate change negotiations are an example of deliberate and ambitious international intervention in the name of sustainable development at the highest scale.

Carbon intensity: fuels which deliver less energy per unit of carbon dioxide emitted in combustion are said to be more carbon intensive.

Implemented properly, this international agreement would cause a discernible and unprecedented shift in the energy–economic relationships that have evolved in the North over the last century. Reliance on fossil fuels would give way to less carbon intensive energy supplies.* Such a shift is perceived as either a threat or an opportunity or both to many governments, industries, groups, traditions, cultures and livelihoods in both developed and developing economies. The framework of the agreement would also affect the present and future livelihoods of the two billion or so people in developing countries who have yet to become dependent on commercial supplies of energy to cook, move and keep warm.

Most human activity uses energy in one form or another and typically in the form of fossil fuel or biomass.* The global supply of fossil fuels is itself finite. The exact finiteness of the Earth's fossil fuel reserves is not accurately known. At current rates of consumption, we have around 40 years of oil, 60 years of natural gas and 230 years of coal left (BP Amoco, 1999). However, new reserves are found each year and recently at around the same rate at which fuel production has been increasing – keeping the so-called reserve/production ratio constant. These reserves are spread unevenly among the world's nations and populations. In a finite world and with rising fossil fuel prices, the geographical unevenness of fossil fuel deposits suggests every likelihood of there being future geopolitical disputes about securing energy supplies.

*Biomass is a collective term for plants and organic matter including: wood and wood wastes; agricultural crops and their waste by-products; municipal solid waste; animal wastes; waste from food processing; and aquatic plants and algae.

A wide range of technological options exists to reduce greenhouse gases. Traditional fossil-fuelled energy supply technologies (e.g. coal and gas-fired power stations) and demand technologies (e.g. cars, lighting, heating and cooling systems) continue to become more energy efficient and therefore less carbon intensive. Meanwhile, new non-fossil fuelled renewable energy technologies and their markets are rapidly emerging in both the North and South as a result of decades of research, development, demonstration and government-led market stimulation.

In many cases advanced cleaner technologies are designed and owned by firms in the North. For this reason the international climate negotiations also focus on the issue of technology transfer from the North to the South. The same issue also arises in other aspects of global environmental change negotiations such as the Convention on Biological Diversity and Agenda 21.*

*The Convention on Biological Diversity was one of the key agreements adopted at the 1992 Earth Summit in Rio de Janeiro. Agenda 21 is a comprehensive plan of action adopted at the 1992 Earth Summit in Rio de Janeiro.

After a decade or so of talking, Northern and Southern developing country negotiators are now seeking ways to operationalize international commitments to enhance the transfer of environmentally sound technologies to the South. A key issue is how to overcome various barriers to the transfer (North–South, South–South) and take-up of advanced cleaner energy technologies, know-how and practices. Various generic types of barriers are said to exist including: lack of capital, lack of appropriate information, inadequate enabling environments and unsustainable (economically) markets, as well as a lack of human and institutional capacities to manufacture, operate and maintain new technologies.

Southern countries frequently voice their concerns that simply buying at a discount or even being given cleaner technologies is unsustainable. Ultimately developing countries seek ways to manufacture such technologies 'endogenously' at home, designing, modifying or re-engineering them to suit local conditions. Cleaner energy technologies are frequently expensive, and designing, building, operating and maintaining them require critical minimum levels of human and institutional capacities. Lack of capital and human capacity to use and maintain new technologies are often cited as key barriers.

Northern countries emphasize the need for the creation of the right 'enabling environments' to engage the private sector and increase the effectiveness of development assistance. They argue that the creation of sustainable markets for new technologies frequently means adapting laws and fiscal regimes, investment in education and training and the development of appropriate institutional capacities.

Under the Kyoto Protocol agreement (see Box 7.1 in the Course Book), Northern countries can meet some of their promises to reduce their own greenhouse gas emissions by 'emissions trading' or by mutual agreement with a developing country partner on a 'clean development mechanism' (CDM) project.*

*At the time of writing (April 2001), the Kyoto Protocol has hit difficulties because the new regime in the US under President George Bush has withdrawn from it.

Emissions trading involves the simple transfer of an amount of greenhouse gas emissions from one developed country's balance sheet to another. Thus, any country that significantly undershoots its 2012 Kyoto Protocol targets (the end of the 'first commitment period') can sell those unused credits to any other country that may be on course to overshoot its domestic target. The downturn in economic activity, coupled with post cold war economic restructuring, has led to a significant reduction in energy use and therefore greenhouse gas emissions in several Eastern European countries. Russia, for example, is highly likely to have 2012 emissions significantly below its Kyoto target and could sell these to a country in the OECD (Organization for Economic Co-operation and Development).*

*The OECD brings together 30 countries sharing the principles of the market economy, pluralist democracy and respect for human rights. The original 20 members are located in Western countries of Europe and North America. Next came Japan, Australia, New Zealand and Finland. More recently, Mexico, the Czech Republic, Hungary, Poland, Korea and the Slovak Republic have joined.

CDM projects involve donor and host partners. Donors providing financial and other backing for the project claim credit for any emissions reductions that can be directly attributable to the CDM project. The host developing country benefits from the project's impact on the transfer of environmentally sound technologies, know-how and practices, capacity building, poverty eradication and contribution towards sustainable development in the region. To date (April 2001) there are no official CDM projects – the institutional mechanisms for their creation are just being settled. CDM projects need to meet the eligibility criteria set out by an 'Executive Board of the CDM' established under the Protocol. In principle, CDM projects can be undertaken in any sector – forestry, energy generation and supply, transportation and domestic energy use – and incorporate a wide range of greenhouse gas reduction technologies such as energy efficiency technologies and renewable energy technologies such as wind, solar photovoltaic and geothermal.

This new and unprecedented approach to international co-operation in global environmental affairs is encountering some severe teething problems. Different stakeholders have different opinions as to what represents a clean, or clean enough, technology for eligibility under the CDM. Proponents of nuclear power argue that it produces relatively few greenhouse gas emissions and so in climate terms is relatively clean. Reforestation and afforestation projects can quickly and relatively cheaply lock up atmospheric carbon dioxide. Opponents to the inclusion of nuclear power and forest projects in the CDM argue that while not formally excluded, such technologies and approaches are fundamentally against the spirit of the agreement and that priority should be given to renewable energy projects instead.

Perhaps more fundamentally, the CDM may, under certain circumstances, lead project participants to overstate the effectiveness of a project at reducing emissions. Donors would receive more credit and host countries would receive more investment, yet the result would be greater emissions than actually claimed. For this reason the need to 'certify' emissions reductions is a key part of what may turn out to be relatively complex institutional arrangements to set up, regulate and monitor the emissions trading and CDM regime.

Activity 16

Let us now try and apply our framework, as depicted in Figure 5.3, to the above account.

(a) What are the sustainable livelihood issues connected to climate change agreements?

(b) What are the sustainable natural resource issues?

(c) What technologies might be involved and why are some of these deemed to be controversial?

(d) What are the institutional arrangements that are outlined for addressing climate change?

(Spend no more than 30 minutes on this activity before reading my discussion below)

Comment

The sustainable livelihood issues are straightforward in that livelihoods require inputs of energy at whatever level we are talking about: domestically for cooking and keeping warm; for transport; and for making a living outside the home. How can livelihoods be sustained and enhanced, yet not be in conflict with ecological sustainability? At a country level there is also an issue of transfer of 'clean' technologies in such a way that it enhances the economic prospects of the country and the livelihoods of its citizens.

The natural resource issues are twofold: the first is assumed throughout the account because it is made explicit in Box 7.1. This is the 'pollution' of the atmosphere by gases, particularly carbon dioxide which is released when fossil fuels are burnt to deliver useful energy, which results in the 'greenhouse' effect and hence climate change. The second issue concerns the possible depletion of fossil fuel reserves and their uneven concentration in the world, together with the possibility of geopolitical wars to gain access to them.

The account indicates that energy technologies are becoming more efficient and, therefore, other things being equal, less carbon dioxide will be released. Also, substitutes for energy technologies that release carbon dioxide are rapidly emerging. The problem is that much of this development is taking place in the industrialized and rich North, rather than the industrializing South, which raises the transfer issue again.

The account also mentions, however, that some technologies that have been suggested as 'solutions' to climate change problems are more controversial. One is nuclear power, which does not release carbon dioxide or any other greenhouse gases, but has its own environmental problems associated with radioactive pollution and the disposal of waste. The other concerns the 'simple' technology of growing trees that absorb and therefore lock up carbon dioxide from the atmosphere. Both nuclear power and growing trees are considered in some quarters to be no substitute for the adoption of benign, renewable, energy technologies.

Two main institutional arrangements are in place for reducing carbon dioxide in the atmosphere. One explicitly adapts market principles and involves trading in carbon dioxide emissions between countries (sometimes pejoratively referred to as trading in 'hot air'). Thus, if country A is failing to meet its internationally agreed carbon dioxide emission-reduction target and country B is more than meeting its emission-reduction target, country A can 'buy' country B's resulting credit. This arrangement is hailed by its proponents as providing a flexible mechanism that encourages countries to reduce their emissions by more than the agreed targets while those who are unable or unwilling to meet their targets can pay an appropriate price for their continuing 'right to pollute'. Those who are against emissions trading argue that it is essentially a charter that enables the biggest polluters, the rich countries, to continue to do so.

The second main institutional arrangement is the 'Clean Development Mechanism' (CDM). In this arrangement, rich countries can claim emission 'credits' at home for clean technology projects that they fund in poor countries. The account above suggests that the main issues here are, firstly, which technologies might qualify for inclusion in CDM projects (see the debate over nuclear power and growing trees above), and secondly how are the emission-reduction claims to be effectively monitored and verified.

Finally at a different level, institutional capacities in Southern countries for making sustainable use of transferred clean technologies, or for developing variants of their own, is raised as an equally important issue.

Waste management and action for sustainable livelihoods in Zimbabwe

This example concerns deliberate intervention for development in the small town of Bindura in Zimbabwe. It is based on research carried out by the main author of this Introduction and by Hazel Johnson, co-ordinator of, and contributor to, the *Poverty and Inequality* Theme.

Bindura (population 30 000–50 000) lies some 90 km north of the capital of Zimbabwe, Harare, and, in common with many similar towns, has a pressing waste management problem. Its population is increasing rapidly due to urbanization processes taking place in Zimbabwe and to general population growth. Associated with urbanization are lifestyle changes which mean that more waste per capita is generated. Meanwhile the waste management infrastructure is deteriorating with broken-down collection vehicles, lack of staff, and a poorly maintained open, unfenced tip just outside the town where the waste is dumped. The tip is perceived to be a health hazard, attracting mosquitoes and vermin, and also human scavengers who pick over the waste for anything of value.

These problems are exacerbated because, along with most countries in the world, the public sector in Zimbabwe does not have the resources to be the sole provider of services such as waste management. In fact, as a low-income country with a structural adjustment programme in place which is targeting the 'efficiency' of the public sector among other things, Zimbabwe has a weaker resource base for providing services than many other countries.

Again, along with most countries in the world, Zimbabwe has sought to limit its public expenditure budget by privatizing services – hiving them off to the private sector. This has been attempted for waste management in several urban areas of the country but the results have not been good, forcing local authorities to take back the services into public ownership in some instances. The main problems have been to do with the capacity of the private sector to do the work and the way in which contracts have been awarded – often as a result of political patronage, rather than by some form of objective criteria (e.g. the lowest tender for the contract in a competitive bidding process).

An alternative to privatization is to seek partnerships with the private sector and 'civil society' (broadly defined to include everything that is not the private sector or the state) to alleviate the problem. This is the preferred approach of the Municipality of Bindura with respect to waste management, and broadly involves participation of the private sector and 'the community' with a strong emphasis on educating the public as to the nature of the problem.

It is within this context that a broad-based ecumenical group in Bindura discussed in 1998 the problem of unsightly waste littering the town as part of an informal weekly class on local social issues. They came up with a novel idea that linked waste management to another pressing issue – that of the livelihoods of the widows of AIDS victims in the town who had become impoverished but who, nevertheless, were trying to raise families. The group wanted to do something for these widows and their families, possibly something that improved their income-earning opportunities. It thus occurred to them to set up a recycling project for the widows, who would earn an income from recycling solid waste such as paper, metals, glass and plastic (see Box 3.4 earlier). Twin concerns such as waste management and impoverishment related to AIDS might then be alleviated in a single project.

The ecumenical group took its idea to a national NGO, based in Harare, called Environment 2000 (E2000). E2000 was sympathetic but believes in working with existing institutional structures and was at that moment nurturing the idea of setting up institutional partnerships on environmental policy in urban areas of Zimbabwe. These partnerships would comprise the local state authority, the private sector and civil society, and would be known as environmental action groups (EAGs).

E2000 suggested, therefore, that the ecumenical group should discuss its proposal with the Bindura municipal local authority, as this body is responsible for waste management in the town. The group did this and there followed a series of workshops which were facilitated by E2000 and involved the local authority, local wings of national ministries (health, education, natural resources), the private sector (the local supermarkets and mining companies were represented), the ecumenical group and other civil society actors. Not present at first, but brought on board for later workshops after representation from E2000, was a local Widows' Association.

Out of these workshops a provisional EAG was formed which would set up the recycling project involving widows of AIDS victims and which would seek donor funding to set the project on its way. The basic idea was that, following an education campaign in schools and via public meetings and posters, residents would separate their waste into two bags – one containing recyclable material and one for everything else. The widows would then collect the recyclable waste by hand carts and take it to a site provided by the local authority. There the widows would separate the waste into its constituent parts (paper, plastic, metal, glass) by hand and be provided with gloves and other protection for this messy job. Finally the separated waste would be transported to Harare and sold.

At the time of writing (April 2001), the project has been running for approximately 15 months and involves 8–10 widows, for whom it is their main cash income source. It would be naive, however, to suggest that the project started without conflict between the various actors along the way. The following are some of the issues that emerged.

There were differences in emphasis about the aims of the project between the local authority and other environmental health professionals on the one hand, and the Widows' Association on the other. The former saw the project as primarily a pilot for more effective waste management; the latter saw it mainly as an income-generating scheme. This affected assumptions about what might happen during implementation. Thus, to the hypothetical question posed at one workshop: 'How would you interpret the situation if only half the predicted number of residents separated their waste?', the environmental health professionals suggested that this would indicate that the community had not been educated enough and more education was therefore necessary. The widows, however, suggested that it might indicate that households were giving the recyclable material to others – local schools, for example, or even to independent entrepreneurs who may have noticed the opportunity. They would therefore request that the local authority pass a by-law giving them an effective monopoly.

There were issues over who should be the 'beneficiaries' of the project. The ecumenical group wanted it to be restricted to widows of AIDS victims who were practising Christians. The local authority said it should be open to all 'poor and needy' widows, drawn from the authority's social register. Private sector members suggested that ability to work hard and make the project a success should also be a selection criterion.

There was ongoing discussion over who should manage the project. Nobody, not even the Widows' Association, suggested it should be the widows themselves, but suggestions ranged from the EAG to the ecumenical group to the local authority. There were also attempts to distinguish between day-to-day management and more strategic issues, such as what to do with any surplus income that was generated (e.g. what proportion should be reinvested) and diversification (e.g. the widows manufacturing some things themselves out of the waste they collected).

The ecumenical group left the project at one stage, complaining that what it had once envisaged as a simple idea under its control had been 'taken over' by other interests. The group came back on board, but the tension remained.

There were also issues relating to the economic sustainability of the project once the donor start-up funding ended. Is there a sufficient market for recyclable waste? Will the project create a satisfactory income for the widows which is at least as good as other potential income sources (such as hawking goods on the streets)?

Activity 17

Now try and apply the framework, as depicted in Figure 5.3, to this cameo.

(a) What are the sustainable livelihood issues of the Bindura project?

(b) What are the sustainable natural resource issues?

(c) What technologies are involved in the recycling process?

(d) Apart from the fact that the waste has to be sold in markets for recycled materials, what is the institutional framework for developing and implementing this project and do you think that this framework is itself sustainable?

(Spend no more than 30 minutes on this activity before reading my discussion below)

Comment

The sustainable livelihood issues of this project are relatively straightforward, at least in economic terms. They can be found in the paragraph immediately prior to the activity. The donor funding is for a limited period and then the project has to be self-sustaining in an economic sense. Of particular importance are the opportunity costs for the widows to be involved. They have multiple sources of potential income activity and the recycling project has to remunerate them at least as well as some of the others.

The sustainable natural resource issues may seem a bit difficult to articulate, because recycling is, by its essence, meant to be a contribution towards sustaining primary resources such as minerals, land and plants, air and water which eventually find their way into consumer goods and their packaging (see Box 3.4 earlier). The raw materials for this particular project, therefore, are not primary resources but the waste products from these consumer goods, and the issue concerns the difficulty for the local environment of absorbing them. Insofar as the project is seen as possibly reducing litter in the town and reducing pressure on the waste tip because it will absorb some of the waste that is generated, it is obviously intended to address this issue. A further question, however, concerns the extent to which the project can make a significant impact – or at least demonstrate that it is possible to make an impact.

The technologies involved are apparently simple: separate bags at household level for distinguishing between recyclable and other waste, hand carts for transporting the recyclable waste bags to a central collection point, protective clothing for separating the waste by hand into its different recyclable components, and motorized transport of the separated waste to Harare.

The institutional framework within which this happens is that of partnership between different actors in the town. Negotiating the terms of this partnership is no easy matter, as the list of issues outlined above testifies. Successful negotiation of these and other issues is, however, key for the institutional sustainability of the partnership.

Thus, one way of looking at this project is that it represents deliberate attempts to create sustainable livelihoods combined with sustainable natural resource use (through recycling) via a sustainable institutional arrangement of partnership between the local state, the private sector and civil society actors.

We can elaborate further on the above Comment by applying the basic criteria that we developed for assessing sustainability in Section 3: continuity over time, robustness, and effectiveness. Thus, in general terms, we can ask whether or not the intervention in Bindura provides for effective livelihoods and maintenance of the natural environment that can be continued over time and not rely on continuing net inputs of aid. We can also apply the criteria more specifically to each of the different elements of the framework, although they will overlap, as we shall see.

The following are some questions we might ask, therefore, in relation to our criteria. The cameo presented does not provide enough information in the main to be able to answer these questions, but what is important here is the realization that all good analysis flows from finding the right questions to ask in the first place.

Sustainable livelihoods: Can the project continue effectively over time, and particularly after the donor funding ends, to support sustainable livelihoods among the participating widows? More specifically, will there be a continuing supply of recyclable waste and can it be effectively (and efficiently) extracted (collected and separated) from the general waste?

Sustainable natural resource use: The question here concerns the environmental aim of the project. Thus, can the project effectively contribute over time to reducing the amount of waste going into landfill?

Sustainable technologies: One set of questions relates to the current technologies. Can they continue to be used over time and do they provide effective extraction of the recyclable waste? Another set relates to bringing in new technologies over time – especially if the answers to the first set suggest that the labour intensity of the original technologies makes the work too hard (and hence not sustainable over time) and does not extract the recyclable waste effectively or efficiently. Bringing in new technologies over time, however, raises the further question of whether the project can create enough of a surplus to invest, or whether this will require further injection of donor funds.

Sustainable institutions: Can the institutional arrangements of partnership between the different stakeholders in the project be effectively maintained over time and without continual 'pushing' by outside actors?

Next, we can use the framework of Figure 5.3 to examine the broad mechanisms by which the project is being managed (as in Section 4). Here our key concepts are *learning* and *accountability*.

So, first we should ask whether or not learning is taking place, and whether or not specific mechanisms such as monitoring and evaluation procedures are in place to enable this to happen, in relation to:

- sustaining livelihoods
- recycling's contribution to conserving the natural environment
- the new institutional arrangements of partnership
- the technologies being employed.

Secondly, we should ask questions about who is learning, how they are learning and what are they doing with their learning, which raises the issue of who holds whom to account. If the different stakeholders in the project are accountable to each other there is the possibility of joint learning and jointly informed decisions on what to do with the learning in terms of the project's development. If the accountability is linear, say from the widows who are doing the work to the environmental action group to the donors, only the last engages in significant learning and they inevitably put their own 'spin' on it.

These learning and accountability questions can be applied to each of the elements of our framework, but they can also be applied to the project as a whole and its contribution to managing broad processes of development (i.e. sustainable development). Here we might want to add *replicability* to our key concepts. Can we learn from this project so that it can be replicated elsewhere? If we have learned from the initial project, any replication is almost certain to be an adaptation of it. Can we continue to learn from the replications and build our knowledge about recycling and sustainable livelihoods?

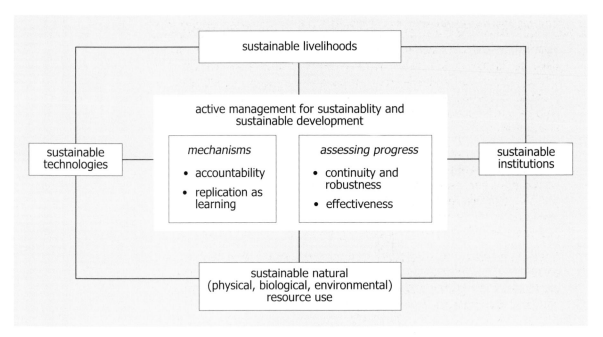

Figure 5.4 Summary map of the main ideas in *Introduction to Sustainability*.

These additional 'ingredients' that we have applied to our framework in relation to the Bindura study are summarized in Figure 5.4. They elaborate upon the framework and, in so doing, they provide a summary map of the main ideas in this text and how they relate to each other.

As a final word on the Bindura project, one might argue that the ingredients are present for it to make a contribution towards sustainable development, but they are not sufficient. Recycling schemes – even if replicated across the whole of Zimbabwe – may be inadequate to make a significant impact on waste generated from continuing urban population growth and lifestyle changes. The institutional arrangements of the project are based on partnership between the local state, civil society and private sector actors, but its livelihood aspects are taking place under capitalism and are hence subject to another set of institutional arrangements – that of markets. There are questions concerning access of the widows to these markets and, in any case, recycling markets tend to be volatile. Meanwhile, the institutional arrangements of partnership fly in the face of long-standing arrangements where the state is supposed to supply services such as waste management and where inclusive arrangements of different social groups, ranging from the local state to private sector to impoverished widows, are hardly the norm.

Summary of Section 5

1 Sustainability and sustainable development are often used interchangeably, but there are differences. Sustainability tends to apply to deliberate development actions, whereas sustainable development is a broader concept that relates to processes of development. Sustainability can also be thought of as means and sustainable development as ends, but, having said that, there is considerable overlap between the terms and these distinctions should not be taken too literally.

2 The classic WCED (Brundtland) definition of sustainable development is a useful starting point, but needs to be given substance because it is so broad. In particular, attention needs to be paid to the ways in which sustainable development may be made to happen, and whose and what needs are addressed, among both present and future generations.

3 It is useful to think of sustainable development as the active management of broad transformation processes in society. The concept of 'management' forces one to identify the goals of sustainable development and in whose interests the process is to be managed, as well as the means of achieving these goals.

4 Sustainable development as active management can be conceived as: (a) direct management of broad transformation processes (e.g. industrialization and globalization); (b) deliberate, positive and sustainable development interventions. In both cases, natural resources are exploited using available technologies and through institutional arrangements to achieve broad goals, such as sustainable industrialization or sustainable livelihoods. This leads to a simple framework for analysing the contribution that active management can make towards sustainable development.

6 Summary of this Introduction and looking forward to Part 2

This *Introduction to Sustainability* has assumed throughout that the concept of sustainability is multi-dimensional, but that all dimensions have certain features in common. Dominant among these common features are continuity over time and robustness, and effectiveness. The last of these is particularly problematic, however, as criteria for effectiveness will differ considerably between different perspectives and standpoints.

Assessing the sustainability of a development intervention is therefore difficult and likely to be disputed. The problem is exacerbated because the different contexts in which sustainability is used cannot be treated in isolation from each other and are best viewed in combination or holistically.

Sustainability can be, and often is, applied to almost any development issue. The Course Book identifies sustainable globalization, sustainable cities and sustainable industrialization explicitly, but also important for development agencies is the concept of sustainable livelihoods.

What draws together these different applications of sustainability is the idea of sustainable development as a management process carried out at different levels. 'Management' is a useful concept because it forces one to confront more specifically goals or needs (e.g. equity and sustainable resource use) that may be disputed by different actors, and to consider strategies for achieving these goals or needs. 'Management' also introduces issues of accountability in attempting to ensure that goals, however broad or narrow, are met and of sustainability or sustainable development as a process of continual learning. With respect to the broad accountability of those who seek to manage big transformations such as globalization and industrialization, a vibrant civil society is seen to be important.

I have ended this Introduction by developing a simple framework for examining the contribution of different actions to sustainable development. It stems from the premise, well articulated in Chapter 7 of the Course Book, that all human activity uses the physical environment as an input to deliver goods and services. The way in which it uses the physical environment depends, however, on the available technologies and institutional structures and it is to these that we must turn if we are to have sustainable use of natural resources allied to sustainable outcomes such as sustainable industrialization or sustainable livelihoods.

This framework has been illustrated briefly above. Part 2 of the *Sustainability* Theme will again apply the framework, concentrating on the management at different levels of one of the three most fundamental natural resources – water (the other two are land and air). By itself, and because of its fundamental importance to life, water is a huge development issue. Human beings use it directly for drinking, for irrigating their crops and sometimes for supplying their energy needs. Access disputes at both local and international levels are frequently close to flashpoint, as are problems associated with its degradation.

Through these detailed studies of different aspects of (sustainable) water management, Part 2 will examine more closely issues only briefly touched by this Introduction – issues of ownership and control, of accountability and of learning for sustainability. It will also apply the framework critically rather than take it as a given. Does it provide us with a useful tool for analysing sustainability or sustainable development? Can we use it in any situation? Or do we need to use it with care and skill, adapting it as appropriate?

References

Allen, T. and Thomas, A. (eds.) (2000) *Poverty and Development into the 21st Century*, Oxford University Press in association with the Open University, Oxford/Milton Keynes [Course Book].

BP Amoco (1999) *Statistical Review of World Energy*, BP Amoco, London.

Blowers, A. (ed.) (1993) *Planning for a Sustainable Environment*, A Report by the Town and Country Planning Association, Earthscan Publications, London.

Brundtland, G. H. (Chair) (1987) *Our Common Future*, The World Commission on Environment and Development (WCED), Oxford University Press, Oxford.

DFID (1998) *Eliminating World Poverty: why the environment matters*, DFID policy statement on the environment, DFID, London.

DFID (1999a) *Livelihoods Approaches Compared: a brief comparison of the UK Department for International Development (DFID), CARE, Oxfam and the United Nations Development Programme (UNDP)*, Department for International Development, London.

DFID (1999b) *Sustainable Livelihoods and Poverty Elimination*, Background Briefing, Department for International Development, London.

DFID (2000) *Sustainable Livelihoods – building on strengths*, Issues Paper, Department for International Development, London.

Edwards, M. and Hulme, D. (1995) 'Performance and accountability: introduction and overview', in Edwards, M. and Hulme, D. (eds) *Non-governmental Organizations – Performance and Accountability: beyond the magic bullet*, Earthscan Publications, London, in association with Save the Children.

Golub, R. and Townsend, J. (1977) 'Malthus, multinationals and the Club of Rome', *Social Studies of Science*, 7, 202–222.

Hurley, D. (1990) *Income Generation Schemes for the Urban Poor*, Development Guidelines No.4, Oxfam, Oxford.

LaFond, A. (1995) 'The sustainability problem', *Sustaining Primary Health Care*, Earthscan Publications, London.

Meadows, D. H., Meadows, D. L., Randers, R. and Behrens, C. (1972) *The Limits to Growth*, Universe Books, New York.

Meadows, D. H., Meadows, D. L. and Randers, R. (1992) *Beyond the Limits: confronting global collapse, envisioning a sustainable future*, Post Mills VT: Chelsea Green.

NPMP (2000) *National Park Management Plan: consultative draft*, Pembrokeshire Coast National Park, Haverfordwest.

Pepper, D. (1984) *Roots of Modern Environmentalism*, Croom Helm, London.

Porteous, A. (2000) *Dictionary of Environmental Science and Technology*, John Wiley, Chichester.

Rahnema, M. (1997) 'Towards post-development: searching for signposts, a new language and new paradigms', in Rahnema, M. and Rowntree, V. (eds) *The Post-development Reader*, Zed Books, London.

Sachs, W. (1997) 'The need for the home perspective', in Rahnema, M. and Rowntree, V. (eds) *The Post-development Reader*, Zed Books, London.

Wallace, D. (1996) *Sustainable Industrialization*, Earthscan Publications, London, in association with the Royal Institute of International Affairs.

Weaver, J., Rock, M. and Kusterer, K. (1997) *Achieving Broad-based Sustainable Development: governance, environment and growth with equity*, Kumarian Press, West Hartford.

Wilson, G. (2000) 'Royds regeneration programme: a case study in inter-organizational relationships', in Robinson, D., Hewitt, T. and Harriss, J. (eds) *Managing Development: understanding inter-organizational relationships*, Sage Publications, London.

Acknowledgements

Grateful acknowledgement is made to the following sources for permission to reproduce material within this book.

Figures

Figure 3.1: © Jeremy Hartley/Panos Pictures; *Figure 3.2 and front cover:* © AP Photos; *Figure 3.4:* © Oxfam; *Figure 3.5:* © Mark Edwards/Still Pictures; *Figure 3.11:* courtesy of the New Economics Foundation; *Figure 5.1:* © Mary Evans/Town and Country Planning.

The Course Team

ACADEMIC STAFF

Joanna Chataway, *Co-Chair and author, Technology and Knowledge*

Jenny Robinson, *Co-Chair, co-ordinator and author, Displacement*

Gordon Wilson, *Co-Chair, co-ordinator and author, Sustainability*

Simon Bromley, *co-ordinator and author, Transitions*

Will Brown, *co-ordinator and author, Transitions*

Pam Furniss, *author, Sustainability*

Tom Hewitt, *co-ordinator and author, Technology and Knowledge*

Hazel Johnson, *co-ordinator and author, Poverty and Inequality*

Bob Kelly, *assessment strategy and author, Study Guide to the Course Book*

Maureen Mackintosh, *author, Transitions*

Judith Mehta, *author, Transitions*

Stephen Peake, *author, Sustainability*

Sandrine Simon, *author, Sustainability*

Alan Thomas, *author and co-editor of the Course Book*

Richard Treves, *author, Sustainability*

David Wield, *critical reader*

Helen Yanacopulos, *co-ordinator and author, Technology and Knowledge*

BBC STAFF

Jenny Bardwell, *Series Producer July 2000–May 2001*

Gail Block, *Audio Producer*

Giselle Corbett, *Production Manager*

Phil Gauron, *Series Producer*

Julie Laing, *Series Personal Assistant*

Andrew Law, *Executive*

Jenny Morgan, *Freelance Director*

Claire Sandry, *Audio Producer*

Mercia Seminara, *Audio Producer*

SUPPORT STAFF

Carolyn Baxter, *Course Manager*

Sylvan Bentley, *Picture Researcher*

Philippa Broadbent, *Print Buying Controller*

Penny Brown, *QA Software Testing Assistant*

Daphne Cross, *Print Buying Co-ordinator*

Sue Dobson, *Web Designer*

Tony Duggan, *Learning Projects Manager*

Peta Jellis, *Course Manager July–November 2000*

Alison George, *Web Designer*

Richard Hoyle, *Graphic Designer*

Lori Johnston, *Editor*

Roy Lawrance, *Graphic Artist*

Cathy McNulty, *Course Secretary*

Katie Meade, *Rights Editor*

Lynda Oddy, *QA Software Testing Manager*

Pauline O'Dwyer, *Course Secretary*

Katharine Reedy, *Library Online Adviser*

Janice Robertson, *Editor*

John Taylor, *Copublishing Manager*

Mark Thomas, *Team Leader, Online Applications Web Team*

Pamela Wardell, *Editor*

EXTERNAL ASSESSOR

Dr K. Bezanson, *Institute of Development Studies, University of Sussex*

CONSULTANTS

Tim Allen, *author and co-editor of the Course Book*

Seife Ayele, *Poverty and Inequality*

Jo Beall, *Sustainability*

Flemming Christiaansen, *Transitions*

Ben Crow, *Sustainability*

Vandana Desai, *Displacement, and Study Guide to the Course Book*

Wendy Fisher, *Technology and Knowledge*

Leroi Henry, *Study Guide to the Course Book*

Ann Le Mare, *Preparing for Development*

Giles Mohan, *Displacement*

Paul Mosley, *Poverty and Inequality*

Njuguna N'gethe, *Study Guide to the Course Book*

Wendy Olsen, *Poverty and Inequality*

Ruth Pearson, *Poverty and Inequality*

Judith Scott, *Poverty and Inequality*

Laixiang Sun, *Transitions*

John Taylor, *Transitions*

David Turton, *Displacement*

Marc Wuyts, *Transitions*

CRITICAL READERS

Henry Bernstein, *Transitions*

Tenkai Bonger, *Sustainability*

Jessimen Chipika, *Poverty and Inequality*

Rachel Marcus, *Poverty and Inequality*

Martin Reynolds, *Sustainability*

Rafal Rohozinski, *Technology and Knowledge*

AbdouMaliq Simone, *Displacement*

WEB TESTERS

Alan Brown, Jackie Bush, Christine Cubbitt, Andrew Dakers, Sarah Downham, Alan Foster, Anna Mattarollo, Fahmida Muhit, Eric Needs, Wendy Shaffer, Nigel Shakespear, Phil Talman

U213
International Development: Challenges for a World in Transition

Course texts

Introduction to Transitions

Introduction to Poverty and Inequality

Introduction to Technology and Knowledge

Introduction to Displacement

Introduction to Sustainability

Transitions

Poverty and Inequality

Technology and Knowledge (web-based)

Displacement

Sustainability